Read on Target for Grades 3 & 4

Student Workbook

Sheila Anne Dean, M.S., CCC-SLP
Jeri Lynn Fox, M.S.
Pamela B. Meggyesy, M.A.
Pamela Marie Thompson, M.S.

Show What You Know® Publishing
Englefield & Associates, Inc.
Columbus, OH U.S.A.

Acknowledgements

Englefield & Associates, Inc., acknowledges the following for their efforts in making this material available for students, parents, and teachers:

Cindi Englefield, President/Publisher
Eloise Boehm-Sasala, Vice President/Managing Editor
Mercedes Baltzell, Production Editor
Scott D. Stuckey, Editor
Lainie Burke, Assistant Editor/Desktop Publisher
Jennifer Harney, Illustrator/Cover Designer
Erica T. Klingerman, Proofreader
Mary Sasala, Proofreader

Published by:
Show What You Know® Publishing
Englefield & Associates, Inc.
P.O. Box 341348
Columbus, OH 43234-1348
Phone: 614-764-1211

www.showwhatyouknowpublishing.com

Copyright ©2002

All rights reserved. No part of this book including interior design, cover design, and icons, may be reproduced or transmitted in any form, by any means (electronic, photocopying, recording, or otherwise) without the prior written permission of the publisher.

Printed in the United States of America
06 05 04 03 02   10 9 8 7 6 5 4 3 2 1

ISBN: 1-884183-83-2

Limit of Liability/Disclaimer of Warranty: The authors and publisher have used their best efforts in preparing this book. Englefield & Associates, Inc., and the authors make no representation or warranties with respect to the contents of this book and specifically disclaim any implied warranties and shall in no event be liable for any loss of any kind including but not limited to special, incidental, consequential, or other damages.

About the Authors

Sheila Anne Dean, M.S., CCC-SLP, received a Bachelor's Degree from Ohio University and a Master's Degree from Miami University. She has worked for ten years in the public schools as a speech-language pathologist. Her work is centered in language development and disorders relating to curriculum. She is currently working as a speech pathologist and supervisor in Ohio.

Jeri Lynn Fox, M.S., holds a Bachelor of Arts Degree from Bluffton College and a Master of Science Degree from the University of Dayton. A Martha Holden Jennings scholar, she has worked in public education for twenty-five years as a classroom teacher and school counselor. In her current role as school counselor, her focuses include improving student achievement and developing supportive parent/teacher partnerships and programming.

Pamela B. Meggyesy, M.A., earned a Bachelor of Science Degree in Education and a Master of Arts Degree in literature from Ohio University. Additionally, she has studied at Oxford University in Oxford, England. A thirty-year veteran classroom teacher in public schools, she has been involved with curriculum alignment and literature selection at the district and county levels. Additionally, she chairs a district-wide writing initiative for her school system. She also has been an instructor at Wright State University.

Pamela Marie Thompson, M.S., has a Master's Degree in counseling from Wright State University and a Master's Degree in school psychology from the University of Dayton. She has taught at the college level and worked as a counselor and program director for a mental health clinic where she supervised case managers and a partial hospitalization program. She is currently employed as a school psychologist. Her background includes experience in testing, assessment, and academic intervention. She has worked in this field for eighteen years. An often sought-after speaker, she has presented numerous workshops dealing with a variety of educational topics including program evaluation and development, behavioral interventions, problem-solving skills, and a concurrent session on instructional planning for the inclusive classroom at the Ohio School Psychologists Association state conference.

The authors have worked together for more than a decade in the Northridge School District in Dayton, Ohio. Their varied educational backgrounds and experiences bring a multifaceted approach to their collaborative educational projects.

©2002 Englefield & Associates, Inc.

Dedication

To our families:

David, Sarah, Marie, Elaine, and Erin, thanks for your love.
Because of you, I truly "enjoy every day." –SAD

Richard, Amy, and Anna, thank you for the joy you bring to my life. –JLF

Joe, Mark, and Lauren; I treasure each of you. –PBM

Nathan, Olivia, and Jason, thanks for your love and encouragement. –PMT

and

To our first teachers:
our parents, by birth and by marriage,
with love and appreciation:

George and Carolyn and Carl and Marianna –SAD

Charles and Edith and Richard and Janice –JLF

George and Connie –PBM

Joe and Emily and Harold and Marie –PMT

Table of Contents

Introduction vi

Activity 1: Analyze Aspects of the Text by Examining Characters 1

Activity 2: Analyze Aspects of the Text by Examining Setting 7

Activity 3: Analyze Aspects of the Text by Examining Plot 11

Activity 4: Analyze Aspects of the Text by Examining Problem/Solution 16

Activity 5: Analyze Aspects of the Text by Examining Point of View 22

Activity 6: Analyze Aspects of the Text by Examining Theme 28

Activity 7: Infer from the Text 32

Activity 8: Predict from the Text 40

Activity 9: Compare and Contrast 49

Activity 10: Analyze the Text by Examining Fact and Opinion 59

Activity 11: Explain How and Why the Author Uses Contents of a Text
to Support His/Her Purpose for Writing 73

Activity 12: Identify Main Idea/Supporting Details 82

Activity 13: Respond to the Text 91

Activity 14: Evaluate and Critique the Text 101

Activity 15: Summarize 110

Activity 16: Cause and Effect 122

©2002 Englefield & Associates, Inc.

Introduction

What is Read on Target?

Read on Target is a book that has 16 reading maps to help you answer tough questions related to something that you have read. *Read on Target* gives students, like you, the tools you need to answer critical-thinking skill questions. Some of these skills include the ability to analyze the story elements, to infer, to predict, and to compare and contrast. You will also need to know how to answer questions like analyze fact and opinion, explain how the author uses contents of the text to support his/her purpose of writing, critiquing, evaluating, summarizing, and determining cause and effect. These are the important thinking skills that are found in this book. Many of these skills teach you how to break down information and to show the relationships in the text. The reading maps in *Read on Target* will guide you, step by step, through the process of answering these types of questions. Each and every reading map is designed to help your ability to reason and to understand what you read.

Why do you need Read on Target?

Sometimes when teachers or parents want to check your understanding of what you have read, they will want to know if you can reason and think critically about information. If you can answer these type of questions, you can show what you've learned. Sometimes it's hard to come up with the right answer when you don't know what they're asking or how to answer the question. *Read on Target* will help you understand how to answer these questions. This will also help you answer tough questions found on many of your tests. By using this book, you'll be more prepared after reading, to answer those questions you know your teachers or parents will ask.

Reading and understanding what you have read are two difficult tasks that you are expected to do for every subject. So, when you know how to read and to understand the text, you can participate in class tasks better and answer those tough questions. You will continue to use these thinking skills as you enter the world of work.

How do you use Read on Target?

Read on Target will guide you through the process of answering critical-thinking questions correctly. *Read on Target* will tell you what to look for when you are reading. You write your answers on the reading map and use your text as you need it. It also helps you practice in your class and lets you see how someone else came up with a good answer. The next time you are asked to answer a critical-thinking skill question, you will be more prepared and better-equipped to provide a complete, well-thought answer.

Activity 1

Analyze Aspects of the Text by Examining Characters

I read to figure out what the characters are like. I get to know them.

Step 1 Read the story "My New Teacher."

My New Teacher

It was Tuesday morning, and it was the first day of school! Mrs. Harrington was eagerly waiting for her students. Her brown, curly hair was always pinned up behind her head. Otherwise, it would have bounced down her back and flopped over her shoulders. Her chestnut brown hair matched the color of her soothing eyes perfectly. She loved children and teaching, and it showed.

As they walked to school, Marcus and Grace talked about how excited they were to meet their new teacher. They had heard that Mrs. Harrington greeted the children with, "Good morning, friends!" They weren't sure how she would greet them today, since it was the first day.

Mrs. Harrington had a way of making every child feel at home. On this first day when the students arrived, she greeted each one with a handshake and said, "Good morning, friends! I'm Mrs. Harrington. It's my pleasure to meet you." The students told her their names and smiled back at her. They did not know where to place their belongings, so one by one she showed them. She knew they might be a little nervous, and she wanted them all to feel comfortable. After she helped them with their jackets and backpacks, she helped each child find a seat.

Marcus and Grace were given seats next to each other near the front of the room. They were even more excited now that they had met Mrs. Harrington, and both were quite curious about what the year in her classroom would be like. Marcus looked at Grace and said, "Wow! Isn't Mrs. Harrington great?"

Grace smiled back at her friend. "She sure is! I bet we get to do all kinds of neat stuff this year."

©2002 Englefield & Associates, Inc.

Activity 1

    The day had started out great! Marcus and Grace knew they would enjoy being in Mrs. Harrington's class. After the children were settled in their seats, Mrs. Harrington asked for helpers to pass out supplies. She walked around the room like a mother cat looking at her new kittens. She knew each child would be able to help in a different way, and she wanted to select the best helpers. She gently tapped Grace on the shoulder. When Grace looked up, Mrs. Harrington asked Grace to go with her to the cabinets. Together, they would find the things everyone needed to begin the new school year. Mrs. Harrington also wanted Marcus to help open boxes. There were lots of jobs on the first day, and Mrs. Harrington wanted everyone to help in some way.

    Mrs. Harrington told her students that she believed every student in her class was very important. She also thought learning was most enjoyable when every student joined in because each of them had ideas to share. Marcus and Grace smiled at each other. They were glad to be in her class!

Activity 1

Step 2: Student Tips

- A character can be a person, a thing, or an object.

- Remember, a character's feelings, actions, and appearance, as well as how other people react to the character, have a huge impact on the events in the story.

- Think about how the story would change if one thing about the character was different.

Step 3: Directions for using Reading Maps 1.1 and 1.2

First: Write the name of the character. (Reading Map 1.1)

Second: Write a sentence from the story next to the description of the character. Cross out any character descriptions that are not found in the story. (Reading Map 1.1)

Third: Figure out what the sentences tell you about the character. (Reading Map 1.1)

Fourth: Read about how the character changed and tell how the story would be different. (Reading Map 1.2)

TITLE I
BEMISS ELEM. SCHOOL

©2002 Englefield & Associates, Inc.

Activity 1

Map 1.1

Analyze Aspects of the Text by Examining the Characters

I read to figure out what the characters are like. I get to know them.

Character's Name: _____

Describe the character.	Write a sentence from the story that tells about the character.	What does this tell you about the character?
What does the character look like?		
How does the character act?		
How does the character feel or think?		
What does the character say?		
What good or bad thing is the character doing?		
How do others react to the character?		

©2002 Englefield & Associates, Inc.

4

Activity 1

Map 1.2 — Analyze Aspects of the Text by Examining the Characters

I read to figure out what the characters are like. I get to know them.

Change the Character.

Change the character to **a teacher who sleeps in class**.
Tell how the story would be different.

_____
_____
_____
_____
_____

Change the Character.

Change the character to **a crying two year old**.
Tell how the story would be different.

_____
_____
_____
_____
_____

©2002 Englefield & Associates, Inc.

Activity 1

| Step 4 | Read the following questions and write your answers. |

1. What kind of person is Mrs. Harrington? Give an example of something she said to support your answer.

   _____
   _____
   _____

2. Mrs. Harrington thinks about how other people are feeling. Based on what you read about her, what does she do that would tell you this?

   _____
   _____
   _____

3. What does it mean when the narrator says, "She walked around the room like a mother cat looking at her new kittens"?

   _____
   _____
   _____

4. How could the story be different if Mrs. Harrington slept in class?

   _____
   _____
   _____

©2002 Englefield & Associates, Inc.

Activity 2

Analyze Aspects of the Text by Examining the Setting

I figure out how important the setting is and how the setting affects the characters and events that take place.

Step 1 Read the story "The Day at the Park."

The Day at the Park

One day last fall, my sister, Kathy, and I went to the park. We decided to go in the early evening because the weather was nice and cool. The sun was sitting lazily on the horizon, and the wind was still. "Wow! What a park!" I said to myself as we rode into the parking lot. The gravel crunched beneath the tires of our bikes. We could see the swings, the slide, and the climbing towers.

We both jumped off our bikes and ran for the swings. We liked to see who could swing the highest before jumping off. As we ran through the grass, it brushed against the bottoms of our pant legs. It had not been mowed recently. Kathy beat me to the swings. She always likes to win! The swings had plastic seats, and the chains squeaked when we moved back and forth. After the swings, we climbed the wooden tower and played "King of the Tower." Then, we slid down the slide. It was a tall, twisting, plastic-covered slide! We hooked our legs and made a train.

After we played on everything, we were tired. Kathy looked at the sky and said, "It's getting dark." The sun was dropping out of sight. The sky looked as if it had been painted with swirls of red, orange, pink, and light purple.

I said, "We better head home. Mom will be worried about us once it starts to get dark." The evening air had turned a little cooler, and dampness had settled on our bike seats. As we rode home, I thought about the great time we had playing at the park. I hoped we could go again sometime soon.

©2002 Englefield & Associates, Inc.

Activity 2

Step 2: Student Tips

- To analyze the setting, you first need to describe the setting.

- Next, think about how the setting affects the story. Let's say you are reading a mystery story. If this mystery story's setting is in a new bright and sunny house instead of a dark old house, it affects the characters and events in the story. The story may be less scary if the setting is in a sunny house.

- You want to think about how the story could be different if the setting changed.

Step 3: Directions for using Reading Map 2

First: **Describe** the setting (where, when, and what the setting looks like).

Second: Tell how the setting affects the characters and events.

Third: Read about **changing what** the setting looks like.

Fourth: Tell how the story would be different.

Fifth: Read about **changing where** the setting is (where the story takes place).

Sixth: Tell how the story would be different.

©2002 Englefield & Associates, Inc.

Activity 2

Map 2 — Analyze Aspects of the Text by Examining the Setting

I figure out how important the setting is and how the setting influences the characters and events that take place.

Describe the setting (where and when the story takes place)

Where the story takes place _____

When the story takes place _____

What the setting looks like _____
_____

Tell how the setting affects the characters _____
_____

Tell how the setting affects the events _____
_____

Now change the setting

Change what the setting looks like to **a park with no slides, swings, or climbing towers.**

Tell how the story would be different. _____
_____
_____

Change where the setting is (where the story takes place) to **Alaska in the winter.**

Tell how the story would be different. _____
_____
_____

©2002 Englefield & Associates, Inc.

9

Activity 2

Step 4
Read the following questions and write your answers.

1. Describe the setting of the story.

   _____
   _____
   _____

2. The park had swings, a slide, and a climbing tower. Explain why this setting had an effect on the story.

   _____
   _____
   _____

3. How would the story be different if the park did not have swings, a slide, or a climbing tower?

   _____
   _____
   _____

4. How would the story be different if it was cold and snowing?

   _____
   _____
   _____

©2002 Englefield & Associates, Inc.

Activity 3

Analyze Aspects of the Text by Examining the Plot

I read to figure out the chain of events; what will happen next.

Step 1 Read the story "Math Class."

Math Class

Listen to this! Have I got a story for you! Yesterday, my friend Carrie and I got in trouble with our teacher. I just cannot believe what happened. We were sitting in math class. I love math; it is my favorite class. I leaned over to help Carrie with a story problem. Story problems are really easy for me, so I thought I would help her. That started the trouble. I told her how to get the answer, and my teacher said I was cheating!

I was not cheating. The rule in our class is we can work on our homework together. It's only important that we know how to get the answer. Our teacher said, "If our friends can help us, then that's OK." However, she said that since we were working during class time, it was not homework. It was seatwork, and she considered what we were doing cheating. Then, she told us to go to the office.

The two of us walked slowly to the office. I decided I would do all the talking. I wanted to explain why we did not think we were cheating. While we waited in the office, I became more upset about the whole situation. After we told the principal the whole story, can you guess what the principal said? He told us to write an apology letter. Writing the letter was hard for us, but we sat in the library and wrote it. After we finished, we handed it to the principal. He smiled and thanked us for taking the time to write the letter. He told us it was important to follow the rule of not working on homework in class.

Finally, we went back to class. Boy, were we embarrassed! I wonder what would have happened if we had refused to write the letter. We learned one big lesson that day–we will never break the class rules again!

©2002 Englefield & Associates, Inc.

11

Activity 3

Step 2: Student Tips

- The plot is the chain of events that happens in the story.

- The plot will have a beginning.

- It will have a rising action, where the events build suspense.

- Next, there is a turning point that leads to the falling action. This turning point is often referred to as the climax. Finally, there is a resolution.

- Think about how the plot affects future actions of the characters and future events in the story.

- As you read, think about how the story would be different if an event changed or was taken out of the story.

Step 3: Directions for using Reading Maps 3.1 and 3.2

First: In the boxes, write the major events (chain of events) in the correct sequence. (Reading Map 3.1)

Second: Read the sentence that tells you which event was changed. (Reading Map 3.2)

Third: Tell how the story is different when one of the events has been changed. (Reading Map 3.2)

Fourth: Read the sentence that tells you which event has been taken out of the story. (Reading Map 3.2)

Fifth: Tell how the story is different when one of the events is left out of the story. (Reading Map 3.2)

Sixth: Write what would happen if the characters' actions were different. (Reading Map 3.2)

©2002 Englefield & Associates, Inc.

Activity 3

Map 3.1

Analyze Aspects of the Text by Examining the Plot
I read to figure out the chain of events; what will happen next.

- First Event
- Second Event
- Third Event
- Last Event

©2002 Englefield & Associates, Inc.

13

Activity 3

Map 3.2

Analyze Aspects of the Text by Examining the Plot

I read to figure out the chain of events; what will happen next.

Change the Plot.

Change the event (writing an apology letter) to happen earlier. How is the story different when this event happens earlier?

_____
_____

Take the event (girls working on homework in class) out of the story. How is the story different when this event is left out of the story?

_____
_____

What would happen if the **characters' actions** changed to **the girls' refusing to write an apology letter?**

_____
_____

14 ©2002 Englefield & Associates, Inc.

Activity 3

Step 4 Read the following questions and write your answers.

1. What happens at the beginning of the story when the girls are in math class?

   _____
   _____
   _____

2. Why did the teacher say the girls were cheating?

   _____
   _____
   _____

3. What could have happened if the girls had completed their homework before class started? How would the story be different?

   _____
   _____
   _____

4. How would the story be different if the girls refused to write an apology letter?

   _____
   _____
   _____

©2002 Englefield & Associates, Inc.

Activity 4

Analyze Aspects of the Text by Examining the Problem/Solution

I read to figure out the problem and how it is solved.

Step 1 Read the story "Anna's Adventure."

Anna's Adventure

"Take your hat, Anna," Mother called as Anna headed for the back door.

"I've got it." Anna replied as she grabbed the red knit hat Grandma had given her for her birthday. Anna remembered how her father had laughed when she first wore the bright red hat.

"Folks will sure see you coming in that hat," he had said. But Grandma said being able to find Anna in a crowd would be a good thing, and Mother had said the hat looked fine, and besides, it would keep Anna warm.

Anna was glad to have her warm red hat. Outdside, it was colder than Anna had expected. She tugged at the zipper on her jacket and pulled it up close to her chin. She then pulled the red hat down to cover her ears and forehead. The autumn air was crisp. The trees had begun to lose their leaves. In the distance, Anna could hear the sounds of tractors and combines working in the fields.

As she was walking near the creek, Anna was greeted by her dogs, Mike and Mattie. "Where have you two been?" asked Anna, laughing. Their muddy paws told her they had been in the creek. Mattie sniffed the air and rubbed against Anna's legs. This was a signal for Anna to scratch Mattie behind the ears. It was a routine Anna knew very well. Mattie wanted the attention first and then she would be on her way to explore foxholes and rabbit nests. Mike was the bigger of the two black Labrador retrievers. His chest was broad, and his face was gentle. Mike was carrying a large stick in his mouth and was wagging his tail. "Do you want to play?" Anna asked him. The big dog dropped the stick at Anna's feet. Just as Anna was about to throw the stick, Mattie's ears perked up. Then she sniffed the air. Before Anna could stop them, the dogs raced into the cornfield. "Wait for me!" cried Anna as she ran after them.

Anna guessed the dogs must be chasing a rabbit, as they were cutting back and forth through the field. Anna was still carrying the stick she was going to throw to Mike when she stopped to catch her breath. The rows where the corn had been planted were uneven and slowed

16 ©2002 Englefield & Associates, Inc.

Anna as she ran after her pets. At first, it was fun to run through the field. The dogs quickly ran out of sight, so Anna used her ears to follow the trail the dogs had taken. Anna's heart was pounding as she drew in deep breaths of the autumn air. Then Anna noticed how quiet it was in the field. She wondered how far she had run. That is when Anna realized she was lost. The corn was almost ready to be harvested, so it was too tall to see over, and the rows were too long for Anna to see where they led. The sun was still shining, but Anna began to feel very cold and very alone.

She called for the dogs, but they didn't come. She could not hear the dogs or any of the sounds from her farmhouse. Anna was working on a rescue plan when she thought she heard people calling her name. It sounded like Mother and Daddy. Anna tried to listen carefully, but she couldn't understand the words they were calling. She only heard the voices, and they sounded far away. Anna had an idea. She carefully bent a cornstalk towards her, then, placing her hat over the tassel tip, she released the stalk. The red hat looked like a flag waving above Anna's head. Before long, Anna could hear Daddy calling, "Anna, I'm coming." Anna wanted to run toward the voice, but he called, "Stay where you are and sing out as loudly as you can." Anna began to sing. Soon, Anna could see the cornstalks parting. She was so happy to see Daddy coming through the corn. Anna hugged Daddy as tightly as he hugged her. Daddy reached up and retrieved Anna's hat from the cornstalk. "That was good thinking, Anna. Mother saw your hat. Your hat led us right to you." Before she took her father's hand for him to lead the way home, Anna pulled on her red hat. It was good to feel safe and warm. Anna decided never to run into the cornfield again.

©2002 Englefield & Associates, Inc.

Activity 4

Step 2 — Student Tips

- Make sure you understand the definitions of a problem and a solution.

- A **problem** is a situation that the character wants to change or something the character wants to do.

- The **solution** can be an action or a decision that helps the character understand how the problem is solved.

- By looking at the character's problems and how the problems are solved, you will be able to follow the events in the story.

- Think how the story would change if the problem changed. When you think about how an event or the solution could be different, you can see how the problem affects the story.

Step 3 — Directions for using Reading Maps 4.1 and 4.2

First: Read the definitions of a problem and a solution. (Reading Map 4.1)

Second: Write the problem of the story that you have read. (Reading Map 4.1)

Third: Write the events that helped solve the problem. (Reading Map 4.1)

Fourth: Write the solution of the story. (Reading Map 4.1)

Fifth: Read about a **different**, made-up problem. (Reading Map 4.2)

Sixth: Write how the **events would be different**. (Reading Map 4.2)

Seventh: Write how the **solution would be different**. (Reading Map 4.2)

Activity 4

Map 4.1 — Analyze Aspects of the Text by Examining the Problem/Solution

I read to figure out the problem and how it is solved.

Read the definition of a problem and a solution.

The **problem** can be:

- A situation that the character wants to change.

- Something the character wants to do or to find out.

The **solution** can be:

- An action that helps the character understand how the problem is solved.

- A decision that helps the character understand how the problem is solved.

What is the problem? _____
_____
_____

What events help solve the problem?

　　　Event 1. _____

　　　Event 2. _____

　　　Event 3. _____

What is the solution? _____
_____
_____

©2002 Englefield & Associates, Inc.

Activity 4

Map 4.2

Analyze Aspects of the Text by Examining the Problem/Solution

I read to figure out the problem and how it is solved.

Change the problem by making up a different problem.

The problem has changed to **Anna following the dogs to a river and getting lost.**

How would the events be different?

Event 1. _____

_____

Event 2. _____

_____

Event 3. _____

_____

How would the solution be different?

_____
_____
_____
_____
_____

©2002 Englefield & Associates, Inc.

Activity 4

Step 4 Read the following questions and write your answers.

1. What is Anna's problem?

   _____
   _____
   _____

2. What events helped Anna solve her problem?

   _____
   _____
   _____

3. How did Anna solve her problem?

   _____
   _____
   _____

4. How would the solution be different if the problem changed to Anna following the dogs to a river?

   _____
   _____
   _____

©2002 Englefield & Associates, Inc.

Activity 5

Analyze Aspects of the Text by Examining the Point of View

I figure out the author's choice of speaker. I also think about why the author chose to write from this point of view and how the story would be different if the story were told from another point of view.

Step 1 Read the poem "Tommy the Slowest Turtle."

Tommy the Slowest Turtle

As Tommy entered his first turtle race,
Everyone there had a very shocked face.
Tommy was tiny, so young and so slow,
The big turtles thought he would not even go.

He was the youngest reptile in the race,
Tommy the turtle walked at a slow pace.
The big faster turtles were set at the gate,
Each turtle walking his fastest of rates.

The race was so long and so tiring and hard,
The big faster turtles moved on, yard by yard.
Each one believed he was one of the best,
And figured he had enough time just to rest.

Those big, fast, old turtles, they stopped and they talked,
While Tommy the turtle continued to walk.
Surprising them all with just what he could do,
Never stopping or talking, just walking on through.

While the big turtles stopped and continued to rest,
Little Tommy the turtle just walked at his best.
Walking and walking, a very slow pace,
Not stopping or talking, he raced, and he raced.

Upon seeing the finish line drawing so near,
That tiny, young turtle soon thought he could hear,
Lots of cheering and clapping and joyful big shouts,
He knew he was winning, without any doubt!

Just then, the big turtles joined in on the fun,
They started to run, and to run, and to run.
While Tommy the turtle kept up his same pace,
That slow, tiny turtle did win the big race!

Activity 5

Step 2: Student Tips

- Make sure you know the definitions and key words of each point of view. You will find the definitions in the Reading Map.

- Think about the reason the author wrote from this point of view.

- Did the author write to let you know what was in the mind of several selected characters only, or did the author let you know what every character was thinking? Perhaps the author told the story to allow you to step into the shoes of the main character.

- Consider how changing the point of view will affect how you feel or think about what you have read. This will give you a clue as to why the author wrote from that point of view.

Step 3: Directions for using Reading Maps 5.1 and 5.2

First: Read the definition and key word pronouns for each point of view. (Reading Map 5.1)

Second: Circle the point of view used in the story. (Reading Map 5.1)

Third: Write one or more sentences from the poem that helped you figure out the author's point of view. (Reading Map 5.1)

Fourth: Tell why the author writes from this point of view. (Reading Map 5.2)

Fifth: Tell how changing the point of view would make the poem different. (Reading Map 5.2)

Activity 5

Map 5.1

Analyze Aspects of the Text by Examining the Point of View

I figure out the author's choice of speaker. I also think about why the author chose to write from this point of view and how the story would be different if the story were told from another point of view.

Point of View	Definition	Key Word Pronouns: They tell the author's choice of speaker.
First-Person	I am in the story. I tell the story.	I, me, my, we, us, our
Third-Person	Someone outside of the story tells the story from what he/she knows.	he, she, they, them
Omniscient (All Knowing)	Someone outside of the story tells the story but knows what everyone sees, feels, and thinks.	he, she, they, them

What is the Point of View?
(circle who tells the story)
1. First-Person
2. Third-Person
3. Omniscient (All Knowing)

Write one or more sentences from the story that helped you figure out the author's point of view.

©2002 Englefield & Associates, Inc.

Activity 5

Map 5.2

Analyze Aspects of the Text by Examining the Point of View

I figure out the author's choice of speaker. I also think about why the author chose to write from this point of view and how the story would be different if the story were told from another point of view.

Why did the author write from this point of view?

Change the point of view to first-person. How is the poem different?

26 ©2002 Englefield & Associates, Inc.

Activity 5

| Step 4 | Read the following questions and write your answers. |

1. What is the point of view of the poem? How did you figure out the point of view of the poem?

   _____

   _____

   _____

2. How would the poem be different if it was told in first-person point of view?

   _____

   _____

   _____

3. Which point of view tells you how everyone thinks or feels?

   _____

   _____

   _____

4. What point of view would an author most likely use if the poem was written as an autobiography?

   _____

   _____

   _____

©2002 Englefield & Associates, Inc.

Activity 6

Analyze Aspects of the Text by Examining the Theme

I figure out the overall message the author is telling me.

Step 1 Read the story "The Gift They Gave Each Other."

The Gift They Gave Each Other

Seven-year-old George liked to play outside. He liked to run and to climb and to hide. Most days, he was covered in dirt. He also watched out for his younger sister, Stephanie. They often played in the sandbox and hid in their fort under the bushes. Their yard touched Mrs. Smith's yard on the north side and was separated from it by a row of apple trees.

Mrs. Smith watched George playing with Stephanie out in the yard and saw them building sand castles. George would help Stephanie fill the bucket and smooth the top before dumping it over. When he thought she was discouraged because the castle was crushed, he patted her back and said, "Your castle is just fine. I'll help you build the walls to make it stronger." When Stephanie got hurt, George put his arm around her to comfort her and got a bandage to make her feel better. It made Mrs. Smith feel good to see George's kindness.

George liked to play pretend musical instruments. He would use buckets for drums and sticks for trumpets. Stephanie sang along with his made-up songs. George always said, "Great job, Stephanie. I loved that song." So did Mrs. Smith! In fact, George's music brightened Mrs. Smith's days. She sat by the window just to hear their voices, laughter, and music.

Some days, George and Stephanie picked wild flowers and apples. They gathered them with care. Then, they would take their treasures to Mrs. Smith. They thought she would enjoy the treasures, but she really enjoyed the children's visits even more!

Last week, George and Stephanie saw a "For Sale" sign in Mrs. Smith's yard. When the children went inside, their mom gave them a note from Mrs. Smith. It read, "Dear George and Stephanie, I have moved to my son's house. I will greatly miss your smiles and laughter. Please continue to share your kindness with others. Love, Mrs. Smith." Mrs. Smith once said how those two children were the brightest part of her life. George and Stephanie never realized their deeds brought kindness to Mrs. Smith. They were so sad when she moved, but they knew Mrs. Smith had been a very special neighbor whom they would miss a great deal.

©2002 Englefield & Associates, Inc.

Activity 6

Step 2 — Student Tips

- Use the Reading Map to help you name some of the ideas that tell what the story is about.

- It will help to skim the text for phrases and sentences that say something about the life of people in general. Look for repeated words or phrases that emphasize important ideas or feelings.

- Think back to events that happened to the main characters.

- Then, think about the lessons that the characters learned.

- Last, think about the main message of the story. Remember the theme is the overall message or major point of the story.

Step 3 — Directions for using Reading Map 6

First: Name some of the ideas from the text that tell what the story is about.

Second: Write the lessons the character or characters learned.

Third: Write a sentence telling what the theme (message of the story) is.

©2002 Englefield & Associates, Inc.

Activity 6

Map 6

Analyze Aspects of the Text by Examining the Theme

I figure out the overall message that the author is telling me.

Name some of the ideas that you learned from the story.

_____
_____
_____
_____
_____

What lessons did the character or characters learn?

_____
_____
_____

Write a sentence telling what you think the theme of the story is.

_____
_____
_____

©2002 Englefield & Associates, Inc.

Activity 6

Step 4 Read the following questions and write your answers.

1. From the idea section of the reading map, write two ideas that you learned from this story.

   _____

   _____

   _____

2. How did the children feel after they read the letter from Mrs. Smith? Tell how you figured out the answer.

   _____

   _____

   _____

3. What lessons did the children learn?

   _____

   _____

   _____

4. Write a sentence explaining the theme of the story.

   _____

   _____

   _____

©2002 Englefield & Associates, Inc.

Activity 7a

Infer from the Text

I read clues and use my knowledge to figure out what is happening in the story.

Step 1 Read the poem "My Two Favorite Seasons."

My Two Favorite Seasons

Can you discover my two favorite seasons?
Think of a summer, fall, winter, or spring day;
See if you're clever, you can find the reasons,
Observing, use knowledge and clues as a way.

What is the first season?

Winter is gone and done,
The snow begins to melt;
By and by, I see the sun,
Gently the warm breeze is felt.

Rain falls in buckets, drips, drops, and showers,
Grass so green when the color comes out,
Yellow, red, and pink blooms on flowers,
Children run, laugh, play, and shout.

What is the second season?

Hot summer sun has faded and gone,
Crisp, clear, fresh air is here;
A cool night's breeze now belongs
To this season, and changes are everywhere.

Teachers are smiling, their students come in.
Soccer and football games with fans to cheer,
Leaves fall to the ground in a swirling wind
As red, yellow, brown, and orange leaves are here.

Activity 7a

Step 2: Student Tips

- When you infer, you need to read the story and **find clues** from the story. Use your **knowledge and experience** to make a guess about what is **happening in the story.**

- As you read the sentences, add new clues to see if your guess is supported by the next clue.

- First, you read each sentence and try to understand its meaning. See if you can find a clue in the sentence. A clue is information in the text that is not directly stated but hints at what the author means. Some students underline or highlight the clues.

- Next, you put the **clues together** with your **own experiences** and make **a guess** about what is happening in the story (this is called an inference). Continue to read more of the paragraph to see if your guess is correct. Now, you can see that sentences and paragraphs build on one another.

Step 3: Directions for using Reading Map 7a

First: Read each sentence of the section to find clues about the meaning of the story.

Second: Write clues from the text in the clue box.

Third: Write about experiences or knowledge you have of a similar thing in the next box.

Fourth: Put together the clues and your experiences or knowledge to make an inference about what is **happening in the story.**

Fifth: Read more of the poem to see if your inference is correct.

©2002 Englefield & Associates, Inc.

Activity 7a

Map 7a

Infer from the Text

I read clues and use my knowledge to figure out what is happening in the story.

My Clues

Find the clues in each sentence or stanza. Write your clues in the boxes below.

Clues to tell you the first season.

Clues to tell you the second season.

+ My Experiences

Think about your experiences and knowledge of a similar thing. Write your information in the boxes below.

Your experiences and knowledge of a similar season.

Your experiences and knowledge of a similar season.

= My Inference

Put the clue and experience/knowledge together to make a guess about what is happening in the poem.

What is the first season?

What is the second season?

©2002 Englefield & Associates, Inc.

Activity 7a

Step 4 Read the following questions and write your answers.

1. What is the first season in the poem?

   _____

   _____

   _____

2. Write a clue from the poem that helped you figure out the first season.

   _____

   _____

   _____

3. What is the second season in the poem?

   _____

   _____

   _____

4. What was your experience or knowledge you used to figure out the second season in the poem?

   _____

   _____

   _____

©2002 Englefield & Associates, Inc.   35

Activity 7b

Infer from the Text
I read clues and use my knowledge to figure out what is happening in the story.

Step 1 Read the story "Animals Everywhere."

Animals Everywhere

One spring day, late in the afternoon, Elaine and Erin were walking home slowly after their long, full day. The sun had risen high in the sky. They watched it continue on its way to evening as it began to dip low toward the horizon. Their legs and feet ached, and their shoulders drooped. They had been walking around for hours and had seen many animals.

When they had first arrived, they had seen two giraffes and an elephant from a distance. The zebras were nearby, too. As the day became hotter, Elaine and Erin went inside some smaller buildings. There were bats and owls in one small building that was dark and cool inside to keep those animals and birds comfortable. The girls also enjoyed the aquarium, which was in another of the small buildings.

Then, they approached a large, outdoor area that contained another familiar animal. There were large bars and a sturdy fence to protect the visitors from him. The four-legged animal roared. He had a big, tan-colored mane. Erin read the sign in front of the fence, which said, "This animal is known as the king of the jungle." The girls were amazed to see him pacing back and forth between the rocks.

"Well, now we have seen all the animals. I sure had fun, but I am getting tired and would like to sit down," said Erin. She added, "It's getting late! We should head home."

"You're right. It's been a long day, and my feet hurt. Let's go!" said Elaine. The girls headed home to tell their families about their day.

Activity 7b

Step 2: Student Tips

- When you infer, you need to read the story and **find clues** from the story. Use your **knowledge and experience** to make a guess about what is **happening in the story.**

- As you read the sentences, add new clues to see if your guess is supported by the next clue.

- First, you read each sentence and try to understand its meaning. See if you can find a clue in the sentence. A clue is information that is not directly stated in the text but hints at what the author means. Some students underline or highlight the clues.

- Next, you put the **clues together** with your **own experiences** and make **a guess** about what is happening in the story (this is called an inference). Continue to read more of the paragraph to see if your guess is correct. Now, you can see that sentences and paragraphs build on one another.

Step 3: Directions for using Reading Map 7b

First: Read each sentence of the paragraph to find clues about the meaning of the story.

Second: Write clues from the text in the clue box.

Third: Write about experiences or knowledge you have of a similar thing in the next box.

Fourth: Put together the clues and your experiences or knowledge to make an inference about what is **happening in the story**.

Fifth: Read more of the paragraph to see if your inference is correct.

©2002 Englefield & Associates, Inc.

Activity 7b

Map 7b

Infer from the Text

I read clues and use my knowledge to figure out what is happening in the story.

| My Clues | + | My Experiences | = | My Inference |

My Clues: Find the clues in each sentence or paragraph. Write your clues in the boxes below.

My Experiences: Think about your experiences and knowledge of a similar thing. Write your information in the boxes below.

My Inference: Put the clue and experience/knowledge together to make a guess about what is happening in the story.

Clues about where the girls are.

↓

Your experiences and knowledge of a similar place.

↓

Where are the girls?

Clues about what the girls saw in the large outdoor area.

↓

Your experiences and knowledge of a similar thing.

↓ ↓

What did the girls see?

38 ©2002 Englefield & Associates, Inc.

Activity 7b

Step 4 Read the following questions and write your answers.

1. What clues told you where the girls are?

   _____
   _____
   _____

2. What experiences or knowledge do you have that helped you infer where the girls are?

   _____
   _____
   _____

3. The text says the girls saw an animal with a tan-colored mane. What did they see? What clues were given to help you infer what they saw?

   _____
   _____
   _____

4. What experiences or knowledge do you have that helped you infer what animal was in the large outdoor area?

   _____
   _____
   _____

©2002 Englefield & Associates, Inc.

Activity 8a

Predict from the Text

I read clues and use my knowledge to figure out what will happen in the future.

Step 1 Read the story "Flying with Monarchs."

Flying with Monarchs

In science class, Sarah and Marie learned about monarch butterflies. They studied what the monarch eats and when it migrates. Sarah loves butterflies because they have such pretty colors and fly so gracefully.

Sarah came home and told her mother all about what she learned. "Mom, did you know monarchs fly from bloom to bloom, landing gently on the petals? Butterflies have mouths that they can use like straws. They use their straw-like mouths to sip nectar from the sweet smelling blossoms. The nectar is the sweet liquid found inside. Nectar gives butterflies energy when they head south for migration."

Marie learned monarchs require warm weather to survive. They migrate south when cool weather arrives. She learned that "migrate" means they move away to find a new home in another place. Marie told her mother, "Some monarch butterflies migrate to warmer places."

To show what Sarah and Marie learned about migration, they drew arrows on the map on the next page. Look at what they learned!

©2002 Englefield & Associates, Inc.

Activity 8a

When monarch butterflies migrate in the fall, they fly south toward warmer climates.

©2002 Englefield & Associates, Inc.

41

Activity 8a

Step 2: Student Tips

- When you predict, you read the story and **find clues** from the story. Use your **knowledge** and **experience** to make a guess about what **will happen in the future**. As you read the sentences, you may be able to add new clues to see if your guess is supported by the next clue. Let's look more closely at the process of predicting.

- First, you read each sentence and try to understand its meaning. See if you can find a clue in the sentence. Some students underline or highlight the clues.

- Next, put the clues together with your own experiences and make a guess about what **will happen in the future** (this is called predicting).

- Read more of the paragraph to see if your guess is correct. Now, you can see that sentences and paragraphs will build on one another.

Step 3: Directions for using Reading Map 8a

First: Read each sentence of the paragraph to find clues about the meaning of the passage.

Second: Write the clues in the clue box.

Third: Write about experiences or knowledge you have of a similar thing in the next box.

Fourth: Put together the clues and your experiences or knowledge to make a guess about **what will happen next** (prediction).

Fifth: Read more of the paragraph to see if the prediction is correct.

©2002 Englefield & Associates, Inc.

Activity 8a

Map 8a

Predict from the Text
I read clues and use my knowledge to figure out what will happen next.

| My Clues | + | My Experiences | = | My Prediction |

My Clues: Find clues in each sentence or paragraph that would help you answer the questions from the passage.

My Experiences: Think about your experiences and knowledge of a similar thing.

My Prediction: Put the clue and experience/knowledge together to make a guess about what will happen next.

Clues about how and what butterflies eat. → Your experiences and knowledge of a similar thing. → Do you think butterflies will eat nuts when they are flying south? Explain.

Clues about the places to which butterflies migrate. → Your experiences and knowledge of a similar thing. → Will butterflies fly long distances when it is time to migrate? Where will they fly?

©2002 Englefield & Associates, Inc.

Activity 8a

Step 4
Read the following questions and write your answers.

1. Looking at the map that Sarah and Marie provided, do you think butterflies from Ohio could migrate to Texas? Explain.

   _____
   _____
   _____

2. What clues from the story helped you figure out whether butterflies could migrate to Texas?

   _____
   _____
   _____

3. Knowing that the butterfly's mouth is like a straw, predict whether or not butterflies will eat nuts when they migrate. Explain your anwer.

   _____
   _____
   _____

4. Predict what would happen to butterflies living in Washington State when fall arrives. Explain your answer.

   _____
   _____
   _____

©2002 Englefield & Associates, Inc.

Activity 8b

Predict from the Text

I read clues and use my knowledge to figure out what will happen in the future.

Step 1 Read the story "The Secret Trip."

The Secret Trip

Carl and David are father and son. They enjoy spending time together and traveling. However, on Saturday, Carl and David are going to go on separate, secret trips. They do not want to tell anyone where they are going because they decided it would be fun to have a contest for their friends and family. The person who figures out where each one is going will get an ice cream sundae, compliments of Carl and David.

Their friends and family made predictions about the trips on notepaper at a gathering last weekend. Here is the information they received about the two trips.

Both men live in the same hometown in Washington State. David's trip is west of his hometown. When David arrives, he will see sailboats in the water. He will also see sand and seashells. David wants to buy a new sketch pad before he leaves for his trip.

Carl's trip is east of home. He will see trees, grass, and flowers high up on the land. He will drive up higher and higher, toward the sky and clouds. When he arrives, he can look down and see the small towns below. The towns look small because he is so high up. Carl will carry his favorite camera with him at all times.

When Carl and David return from their trips, they will invite their friends and family over again. Each man will tell the group where he went and what he saw. Then, David will take out the notepaper and will check to see who had the correct answers. They are certain that Marianna will have the correct answers and will win the prize, because she's been married for 40 years to her wonderful husband, Carl, and David, at 37 years old, is her oldest son. She has spent a lot of time with them and knows a lot about these two special people in her life!

©2002 Englefield & Associates, Inc.

Activity 8b

Step 2: Student Tips

- When you predict, you read the story and **find clues** from the story. Use your **knowledge** and **experience** to make a guess about what **will happen in the future**. As you read the sentences, you may be able to add new clues to see if your guess is supported by the next clue. Let's look more closely at the process of predicting.

- First, you read each sentence and try to understand its meaning. See if you can find a clue in the sentence. Some students underline or highlight the clues.

- Next, put the clue together with your own experiences and make a guess about what **will happen in the future** (this is called predicting).

- Read more of the paragraph to see if your guess is correct. Now, you can see that sentences and paragraphs will build on one another.

Step 3: Directions for using Reading Map 8b

First: Read each sentence of the paragraph to find clues about the meaning of the passage.

Second: Write the clues in the clue box.

Third: Write about experiences or knowledge you have of a similar thing in the next box.

Fourth: Put together the clues and your experiences or knowledge to make a guess about **what will happen next** (prediction).

Fifth: Read more of the paragraph to see if the prediction is correct.

©2002 Englefield & Associates, Inc.

Activity 8b

Map 8b

Predict from the Text

I read clues and use my knowledge to figure out what will happen next.

| My Clues | + | My Experiences | = | My Prediction |

Find clues in each sentence or paragraph that would help you answer the questions from the passage.

Think about your experiences and knowledge of a similar thing.

Put the clue and experience/knowledge together to make a guess about what will happen next.

Clues about where David will go and what he will take with him.

→ Your experiences and knowledge of a similar thing.

→ What will David bring home from his trip?

Clues about where Carl will go and what he will take with him.

→ Your experiences and knowledge of a similar thing.

→ What will Carl bring home from his trip?

©2002 ENGLEFIELD & ASSOCIATES, Inc.

47

Activity 8b

Step 4 Read the following questions and write your answers.

1. What will David bring home from his trip? What clues helped you predict this?

   _____
   _____
   _____

2. After reading about where David will go on his trip, what are your experiences and knowledge of a similar thing?

   _____
   _____
   _____

3. Why will Carl take his favorite camera on his trip?

   _____
   _____
   _____

4. What will Carl bring home from his trip? Tell how you figured out your answer.

   _____
   _____
   _____

©2002 Englefield & Associates, Inc.

Activity 9a

Compare and Contrast
I read to find out how two or more things are alike and different.

Step 1 Read the story "Kitchens: Past and Present."

Kitchens: Past and Present

Hannah, Michael, Samantha, and Joey were helping their mother make cookies. Hannah asked, "Mommy, were kitchens always like this?"

"No, Hannah, kitchens have changed a lot through the years. For example, kitchens of the early 1900s were usually smaller, and they were very often a square shape. The floors were usually covered with a rubbery material called linoleum that you would need to wax and to buff to keep it looking nice. The stove was usually made of black iron and was heated with wood. The refrigerator, called an icebox, was much smaller than today's and was kept on the back porch rather than in the kitchen. Kitchens were much quieter without the sound of electric appliances. You would hear the sounds of the mother chopping, mixing and stirring food by hand. The stove would have a crackling noise as a wood fire heated the food. You would also hear the splash of water as dishes were washed in the sink, and you would hear the footsteps of the iceman as he put a big block of ice into the icebox. That is why they were called iceboxes."

Joey said, "Gee, our kitchen looks much different today. It is really big and is a rectangle shape with an oval place for the table. I like our wood floor because it is easy to clean by just damp mopping instead of all that work on the linoleum floor."

The children's mother agreed. "Yes, there are lots of choices for floors today, like tile, carpet, wood, and vinyl. People today want products that are easy to take care of because they just don't have the time at home like people did long ago. We don't have to build a fire in our electric stove to get it to heat up either, and I prefer its white color to the old black iron wood stoves. Now that refrigerators don't need to have a real ice block to remain cold, they have

©2002 Englefield & Associates, Inc.

Activity 9a

much more room in them for food and stay much colder. I guess one bad thing about kitchens today is they are noisier. You can hardly talk over the loud motors of the electric can opener, blender, and mixer. Even the microwave oven makes a whirring noise as the food heats inside. The swish of water in the dishwasher as it washes the dishes is loud, too."

Michael replied, "What about the icemaker when it fills and drops the ice in the bin? Sometimes it startles me like somebody is dropping something in the kitchen."

"Yes, the kitchen of the past was much different than that of today," their mother said. "We still cook and eat food in the kitchen, but, oh boy, how things have changed."

Activity 9a

Step 2: Student Tips

- The key to figuring out how something is alike or different is first to describe the characteristics of each item.

- After you have described each of the characteristics, you will be able to see how each characteristic is either alike or different.

- When you compare, you are determining how two or more things are alike or the same.

- When you contrast, you are determining how two or more things are different.

Step 3: Directions for using Reading Map 9a

First: Write the names of the things to be compared and contrasted in the shaded boxes.

Second: Describe the characteristics of the things to be compared and contrasted. A blank box is provided for you to write your own characteristic to be compared and contrasted.

Third: If the items have the **same** characteristic, put a plus sign (+) in the box under the shaded boxes and next to the "Describe the Characteristic" box.

Fourth: If the items have **different** characteristics, put a minus sign (−) in the box under the shaded boxes and next to the "Describe the Characteristic" box.

You may not need all the descriptive boxes. Cross out any descriptions you are not able to find after reading the text.

©2002 Englefield & Associates, Inc.

Activity 9a

Map 9a

Compare and Contrast

I read to figure out how two things are alike and different.

Directions: How would you describe the things that you are going to compare and contrast? What shape are they? What color are they? Etc. Put a plus sign (+) in a box that matches a characteristic of the other items. Put a minus sign (–) in a box that doesn't match a characteristic of the other items.

Describe the Characteristics. Tell what the things look like. Write your answer in the box next to these characteristics. (Under the shaded boxes.)	Write the names of the things that you are going to compare and contrast in the three shaded boxes below.			
Shape		+ or –	+ or –	+ or –
Color		+ or –	+ or –	+ or –
Size		+ or –	+ or –	+ or –
It is...		+ or –	+ or –	+ or –
Sounds like...		+ or –	+ or –	+ or –
Feels like...		+ or –	+ or –	+ or –
Write your own characteristic to compare and contrast.		+ or –	+ or –	+ or –

©2002 Englefield & Associates, Inc.

Activity 9a

Step 4 Read the following questions and write your answers.

1. How do people cook differently today than in the past?

   _____
   _____
   _____

2. How is the size of a kitchen different today than in the past?

   _____
   _____
   _____

3. How are the sounds in the kitchen of the past different than in the kitchen of the present?

   _____
   _____
   _____

4. What things do people do with their stoves that are the same today as in the past?

   _____
   _____
   _____

©2002 Englefield & Associates, Inc.

Activity 9b

Compare and Contrast

I read to find out how two or more things are alike and different.

Step 1 Read the story "Apples and Oranges."

Apples and Oranges

Mark and Lauren sat in their kitchen watching their mother dig the seeds out of an apple to prepare it for a fruit salad. Lauren thought its round shape was pretty and enjoyed looking at the different colors of apples that her mother had selected for the fruit dish. Most of all, she especially enjoyed their flavors.

Both oranges and apples were used in the fruit salad. They were the size of baseballs. Their mother had started with round oranges, which she peeled carefully and then pulled the sections apart. Then, she used large, round apples. When she cut the apples, they made a crisp, swishing sound. The oranges hardly made any noise at all.

Mark said, "Please put more oranges into the fruit salad, Mom. I love the way the orange color makes the fruit salad so beautiful. Besides, I want to use the rind for my fake smile. I like the way the rind feels so soft and bumpy at the same time."

"Why do you like oranges so much, Mark?" Lauren asked.

"Well," he answered, "let me think. I guess I like their round shape. I also like how they feel chewy when the pulp squishes in my mouth. Oranges have a taste that has a sweetness and a tartness at the same time. Sometimes, they even make my mouth pucker. And I really like the way you can smell oranges with that same sweet, citrus smell. And besides," he added, "they taste the best of all the fruit."

Activity 9b

Lauren said, "I like apples better. They feel really smooth on the outside, and when you bite into good juicy ones, they almost squirt. Plus, they come in different colors and look really pretty in the salad. See, Mom put in yellow, red, and green ones, and they all have slightly different tastes. They can taste sweet or tart. Apples smell tart like apple cider, and I like the way they are crunchy when you bite into them. And look at the fruit salad. The pieces of red apple look the prettiest, like jewels tucked in among all the other fruits."

"Mom, which do you think is better?"

Their mom looked up and said, "Plums."

TITLE I
BEMISS ELEM. SCHOOL

©2002 Englefield & Associates, Inc.

Activity 9b

Step 2: Student Tips

- The key to figuring out how something is alike or different is first to describe the characteristics of each item.

- After you have described each of the characteristics, you will be able to see how each characteristic is either alike or different.

- When you compare, you are determining how two or more things are alike or the same.

- When you contrast, you are determining how two or more things are different.

Step 3: Directions for using Reading Map 9b

First: Write the names of the things to be compared and contrasted in the shaded boxes.

Second: Describe the characteristics of the things to be compared and contrasted. A blank box is provided for you to write your own characteristic to be compared and contrasted.

Third: If the items have **same** characteristic, put a plus sign (+) in the box under the shaded boxes and next to the "Describe the Characteristic" box.

Fourth: If the items have **different** characteristics, put a minus sign (–) in the box under the shaded boxes and next to the "Describe the Characteristic" box.

You may not need all the descriptive boxes. Cross out any descriptions you are not able to find after reading the text.

©2002 Englefield & Associates, Inc.

Activity 9b

Map 9b

Compare and Contrast

I read to figure out how two things are alike and different.

Directions: How would you describe the things that you are going to compare and contrast? What shape are they? What color are they? Etc. Put a plus sign (+) in a box that matches a characteristic of the other items. Put a minus sign (–) in a box that doesn't match a characteristic of the other items.

Describe the Characteristics. Tell what the things look like. Write your answer in the box next to these characteristics. (Under the shaded boxes.)	Write the names of the things that you are going to compare and contrast in the three shaded boxes below.		
Shape	+ or –	+ or –	+ or –
Color	+ or –	+ or –	+ or –
Size	+ or –	+ or –	+ or –
Is made of...	+ or –	+ or –	+ or –
Sounds like...	+ or –	+ or –	+ or –
Feels like...	+ or –	+ or –	+ or –
Write your own characteristic to compare and contrast.	+ or –	+ or –	+ or –

©2002 Englefield & Associates, Inc.

57

Activity 9b

Step 4
Read the following questions and write your answers.

1. Compare the shape of an orange with the shape of an apple.

   _____
   _____
   _____

2. An apple is described as "smooth on the outside," and an orange is described as "soft and bumpy." Is this a comparison or a contrast? Why?

   _____
   _____
   _____

3. How are the sizes of an apple and an orange alike?

   _____
   _____
   _____

4. Contrast the smell of an apple with the smell of an orange.

   _____
   _____
   _____

©2002 Englefield & Associates, Inc.

Activity 10a

Analyze the Text by Examining the Use of Fact and Opinion

I figure out if the reading is something that can be proven by evidence or if the reading is a personal belief that tells how someone feels or thinks about something.

Step 1 Read the story "Caving."

Caving

My friend Amy and I were sure that caving camp would be the most exciting summer experience we could plan. The thought of crawling through caves with a few friends to see nature sounded like fun. We learned many things about this activity at our caving camp. The formal name for this activity is spelunking, and those who explore caves are called spelunkers. Most of my friends just call it caving.

Before we arrived at caving camp, we spent time gathering old clothes to wear in the caves. Old jeans, T-shirts, flannel shirts, and coveralls make great caving clothes. Dressing in layers is a must for caving. The guides at caving camp wear at least two pair of socks, sturdy work boots, and gloves.

Our counselor told us the temperature of a cave stays the same all year. A good rule to figure out how cold it will be in the cave is to find the midpoint between the area's hottest temperature in summer and its coldest temperature in winter. Our caves were about 54 degrees all year. Once you know the cave's temperature, you can plan how many layers of clothes to wear.

At camp, we learned that wearing a hard hat is a good idea for safety. We carried flashlights, extra batteries, and bulbs. A good flashlight attached to a helmet will light the underground caverns and allows the caver to keep both hands free for getting through the cave. When people go caving, they carry waterproof backpacks so they can carry gear and still use both hands for climbing and crawling.

The safest way to explore a cave is to travel in a team of at least four people. In case someone gets injured, one person can stay with the person who is hurt and two people can go together to get help. Before the team starts to explore a cave, they should always check in with a park ranger to let someone know they are going into the cave.

©2002 Englefield & Associates, Inc.

Activity 10a

To protect the natural beauty of a cave, cavers should never leave anything in a cave. Cavers should always carry out everything they carry in. This includes their trash.

We learned that cavers get covered in mud. People should never be afraid to get dirty if they want to explore caves. They also must be willing to crawl through small openings in the rock walls in the dark. Most of all, we learned caving is a great activity for all people who like a challenge. Everyone should try caving!

Step 2: Student Tips

- **Facts** are things that can be proven by evidence or observation. You can check the information by looking it up or seeing it. Facts are true for everyone.

- **Opinions** tell personal beliefs or judgments about something. Sometimes, an opinion has a key word that describes or overstates something. Examples of some opinion key words are best, great, and beautiful. Some words that overstate opinions are always, never, and everyone. Opinions are true for some people.

- Read more about key words in the **Fact and Opinion Worksheet** (Map 10a.3). On the same worksheet, practice writing fact sentences and changing them to opinion sentences by adding key words.

©2002 Englefield & Associates, Inc.

Activity 10a

| Step 3a | **Directions for using Reading Maps 10a.1 and 10a.2** |

First: Write a sentence or sentences from the text that tell you whether the story is a fact or an opinion.

Second: Think how the sentences are supported by facts or opinions.

Third: If the sentences tell you that the reading material is a fact, then use the left side to:

- Write how the information can be proven by evidence or observation.
- Write where you would check for information or where you would see it.
- Tell if the information is true for everyone.

OR

Third: If the sentences tell that the reading material is an opinion, then use the right side to:

- Write KEY WORDS that are clues to tell how someone thinks or feels.
- Write how the information tells a personal belief or judgment about something.
- Tell if the information is true for some people.

Fourth: Now, use Map 10a.2 to find sentences that support the opposite perspective (fact or opinion).

| Step 3b | **Directions for using the Fact and Opinion Worksheet (Reading Map 10a.3)** |

First: Read the definitions of a fact and an opinion.

Second: Read the examples of KEY WORDS.

Third: Practice changing a fact into an opinion.

- Write a fact sentence.
- Add a KEY WORD to change the fact into an opinion.

Fourth: Practice changing an opinion into a fact.

- Write an opinion sentence using a KEY WORD.
- Take the KEY WORD out of the sentence and write a fact sentence.

©2002 Englefield & Associates, Inc.

Activity 10a

Map 10a.1 Analyze Aspects of the Text by Examining the Use of Fact and Opinion

I read to figure out if the reading is something that can be proven by evidence or observation or if the reading is a personal belief that tells how someone feels or thinks about something.

Write a sentence or sentences from what you read.

_____
_____
_____

⟵ OR ⟶

If you think the sentence is a FACT, then:

Write how the information that you read can be proven by evidence or observation.
_____
_____

Write where you would check by looking up the information or where you would see it.
_____
_____

Is the information true for everyone? _____

If you think the sentence is an OPINION, then:

Write the KEY WORDS, which are clues that tell you how someone thinks, feels, or overstates.
_____
_____

Write how the information tells a personal belief or judgment about something.
_____
_____

Is the information true for some people? _____

62 ©2002 Englefield & Associates, Inc.

Activity 10a

Map 10a.2 Analyze Aspects of the Text by Examining the Use of Fact and Opinion

I read to figure out if the reading is something that can be proven by evidence or if the reading is a personal belief that tells how someone feels or thinks about something.

Write a sentence or sentences from what you read.

_____

———— OR ————

If you think the sentence is a FACT, then:

Write how the information that you read can be proven by evidence or observation.
_____
_____
_____

Write where you would check by looking up the information or where you would see it.
_____
_____

Is the information true for everyone? _____

If you think the sentence is an OPINION, then:

Write the KEY WORDS, which are clues that tell you how someone thinks, feels, or overstates.
_____
_____
_____

Write how the information tells a personal belief or judgment about something.
_____
_____

Is the information true for some people? _____

©2002 Englefield & Associates, Inc.   63

Activity 10a

Map 10a.3 — Fact and Opinion Worksheet

Facts	Opinions
• true for everyone • can be proven and supported by evidence and observation • can be checked by looking up the information or seeing it	• true for some people • tells how someone thinks or feels about something • personal belief or judgment about something

You can use key words to change a fact into an opinion. Here are some examples of key words that will help you figure out if the information is an opinion.

KEY WORDS that describe an opinion:
best, great, easy, hard, beautiful, pretty, good, bad, difficult, ugly, terrible, excellent

KEY WORDS that overstate an opinion:
always, never, all, everyone

FACT + KEY WORD = OPINION

Here is an example: 1. This is a book. (fact)
2. This is a great book. (opinion)

Practice changing a fact into an opinion.

Write a fact sentence: _____

Add a KEY WORD to change the fact into an opinion: _____
_____

Practice changing an opinion into a fact.

Write an opinion sentence (remember to use a KEY WORD): _____
_____

Take the KEY WORD out of the opinion sentence and write a fact sentence: _____
_____

©2002 Englefield & Associates, Inc.

Activity 10a

> **Step 4** Read the following questions and write your answers.

1. To protect the natural beauty of a cave, cavers should never leave anything in the cave. Is this a fact or an opinion? Explain your answer.

   _____
   _____
   _____

2. The cavers were covered in mud. Is this a fact or an opinion? Explain your answer.

   _____
   _____
   _____

3. Write one factual sentence from the story that describes what the guides at caving camp wear.

   _____
   _____
   _____

4. Write an opinion sentence from the story. Explain why this is an opinion.

   _____
   _____
   _____

©2002 Englefield & Associates, Inc.

Activity 10b

Analyze the Text by Examining the Use of Fact and Opinion

I figure out if the reading is something that can be proven by evidence or if the reading is a personal belief that tells how someone feels or thinks about something.

Step 1 Read the story "The Weather Chart."

The Weather Chart

The weather certainly determines where children can play. For instance, Mike, Sue, and Sam are cousins who like to play together. Since it is July, they play outside. They are allowed to ride their bikes to the swimming pool. They enjoy playing tag with their friends in the neighborhood and selling lemonade to people who walk by. Sometimes, they get out their chalk to draw animals, to trace their bodies, and to draw hopscotch boards on the sidewalk. They think there's so much more to do outside than inside.

When they play inside, they have to stay quiet and calm. They try to stay "as cool as cucumbers." It is easy for the children to stay quiet. They play games like cards and checkers. They sometimes play school. If they know they'll be inside for a long time, they start a hard puzzle. Sometimes, they make crazy creations with clay.

Some days, the children can choose where they want to play, but on other days, the weather makes it hard to plan whether they'll play inside or outside. On Monday, Mike, Sue, and Sam weren't sure about the weather. They decided to check the newspaper to see what the weather would be like for the next few days so they could plan where they would play. Sue looked in the paper for a weather chart. "Weather charts always give you correct information," she said. She found a chart called "An Easy-to-Use Weather Chart."

After looking at the chart, Mike planned to set up his indoor games Tuesday night. The chart said it would rain on Wednesday. He said, "The weather chart is easy for everyone to use. This chart is a good way to plan your day."

©2002 Englefield & Associates, Inc.

Activity 10b

An Easy-to-Use Weather Chart

Today/Monday	Tuesday	Wednesday	Thursday	Friday
Partly sunny	Sunny and hot	Rain showers	Cloudy	Sunny and warm

Step 2 Student Tips

- **Facts** are things that can be proven by evidence or observation. You can check the information by looking it up or seeing it. Facts are true for everyone.

- **Opinions** tell personal beliefs or judgments about something. Sometimes, an opinion has a key word that describes or overstates something. Examples of some opinion key words are best, great, and beautiful. Some words that overstate opinions are always, never, and everyone. Opinions are true for some people.

- Read more about key words in the **Fact and Opinion Worksheet** (Map 10b.3). On the same worksheet, practice writing fact sentences and changing them to opinion sentences by adding key words.

©2002 Englefield & Associates, Inc.

Activity 10b

Step 3a: Directions for using Reading Maps 10b.1 and 10b.2

First: Write a sentence or sentences from the text that tell you whether the story is a fact or an opinion.

Second: Think how the sentences are supported by facts or opinions.

Third: If the sentences tell you that the reading material is a fact, then use the left side to:
- Write how the information can be proven by evidence or observation.
- Write where you would check for information or where you would see it.
- Tell if the information is true for everyone.

OR

Third: If the sentences tell that the reading material is an opinion, then use the right side to:
- Write KEY WORDS that are clues to tell how someone thinks or feels.
- Write how the information tells a personal belief or judgment about something.
- Tell if the information is true for some people.

Fourth: Now, use Map 10b.2 to find sentences that support the opposite perspective (fact or opinion).

Step 3b: Directions for using the Fact and Opinion Worksheet (Reading Map 10b.3)

First: Read the definitions of a fact and an opinion.

Second: Read the examples of KEY WORDS.

Third: Practice changing a fact into an opinion.
- Write a fact sentence.
- Add a KEY WORD to change the fact into an opinion.

Fourth: Practice changing an opinion into a fact.
- Write an opinion sentence using a KEY WORD.
- Take the KEY WORD out of the sentence and write a fact sentence.

Activity 10b

Map 10b.1 Analyze Aspects of the Text by Examining the Use of Fact and Opinion

I read to figure out if the reading is something that can be proven by evidence or if the reading is a personal belief that tells how someone feels or thinks about something.

Write a sentence or sentences from what you read.

_____

⟵ OR ⟶

If you think the sentence is a FACT, then:

Write how the information that you read can be proven by evidence or observation.

_____
_____
_____

Write where you would check by looking up the information or where you would see it.

_____
_____
_____

Is the information true for everyone? _____

If you think the sentence is an OPINION, then:

Write the KEY WORDS, which are clues that tell you how someone thinks, feels, or overstates.

_____
_____
_____

Write how the information tells a personal belief or judgment about something.

_____
_____
_____

Is the information true for some people? _____

©2002 Englefield & Associates, Inc.

69

Activity 10b

Map 10b.2 Analyze Aspects of the Text by Examining the Use of Fact and Opinion

I read to figure out if the reading is something that can be proven by evidence or if the reading is a personal belief that tells how someone feels or thinks about something.

Write a sentence or sentences from what you read.

_____

← OR →

If you think the sentences tell you the reading is a FACT, then:

Write how the information that you read can be proven by evidence or observation.

_____

Write where you would check by looking up the information or where you would see it.

_____

Is the information true for everyone? _____

If you think the sentences tell you the reading is an OPINION, then:

Write the KEY WORDS, which are clues that tell you how someone thinks, feels, or overstates.

_____

Write how the information tells a personal belief or judgment about something.

_____

Is the information true for some people? _____

©2002 Englefield & Associates, Inc.

Activity 10b

Map 10b.3 — Fact and Opinion Worksheet

Facts
- true for everyone
- can be proven and supported by evidence and observation
- can be checked by looking up the information or seeing it

Opinions
- true for some people
- tells how someone thinks or feels about something
- personal belief or judgment about something

You can use key words to change a fact into an opinion. Here are some examples of key words that will help you figure out if the information is an opinion.

KEY WORDS that describe an opinion:
best, great, easy, hard, beautiful, pretty, good, bad, difficult, ugly, terrible, excellent

KEY WORDS that overstate an opinion:
always, never, all, everyone

FACT + KEY WORD = OPINION

Here is an example: 1. This is a book. (fact)
2. This is a great book. (opinion)

Practice changing a fact into an opinion.

Write a fact sentence: _____

Add a KEY WORD to change the fact into an opinion: _____
_____

Practice changing an opinion into a fact.

Write an opinion sentence (remember to use a KEY WORD): _____
_____

Take the KEY WORD out of the opinion sentence and write a fact sentence: _____
_____

©2002 Englefield & Associates, Inc.

Activity 10b

> **Step 4** Read the following questions and write your answers.

1. Write two opinions from the text.

   _____
   _____
   _____

2. The chart said it would rain on Wednesday. Is this statement a fact or an opinion? Explain your answer.

   _____
   _____
   _____

3. The weather chart is easy for everyone to use. This chart is a good way to plan everyone's day. Are these sentences facts or opinions? Explain your answer.

   _____
   _____
   _____

4. Write two facts from the story that tell you what the children might do on Wednesday if it rains.

   _____
   _____
   _____

Activity 11a

Explain How and Why an Author Uses Contents of a Text to Support His/Her Purpose for Writing

I tell the process (how) and the reason (why) the story was written.

Step 1 Read the story "Expect Something Good to Happen."

Expect Something Good to Happen

Mario sighed and stared out the window. Since the doctor had set his cast, his arm ached only a little, but that fractured arm sure was hurting the plans Mario had made for the summer. Six weeks with no swimming, no baseball, and no summer camp would be a real pain. By the time his arm healed, summer would be almost over. Mario sighed again. It had been an awful day.

"I'm going for a walk," announced Lionel. "Want to come along?" Mario knew his older brother was trying to cheer him up, but Mario was too sad to be cheered up. He was sure his summer was ruined. "What's the point?" Mario replied. Lionel understood how disappointed Mario was feeling. He said, "Well, there just might be a bright side to your situation if you would be open to new possibilities."

Mario had heard his parents and grandparents say the same thing many times. Looking for something good to come from a difficult or disappointing situation was a family motto. Mario could not imagine how anything good could come from his broken arm, but he decided to go with his brother anyway.

The boys were barely at the end of their driveway when they saw their neighbor, Mr. Nathan. Mr. Nathan was a nice man who usually walked his dog, Zoey, early in the morning. He was walking a new dog this evening. "Nice dog, Mr. Nathan. But where is Zoey?" asked Lionel.

"Zoey is at home, resting. I found this young pup wandering near the highway. She seemed lost and hungry," said the kind man. He went on to tell the boys how he had checked the animal shelter and had placed an ad in the newspaper. No one seemed to know where the spotted dog belonged. "It's too bad. This dog needs a good home. But I only have enough time to care for one dog," Mr. Nathan continued. "This is a really nice dog. She is smart, too. She knows several tricks, and I am sure she could learn more if someone had the time to work with her," he added. Mario had always wanted to have a dog, but with all his sports and camping activities, he didn't have time to care for one.

©2002 Englefield & Associates, Inc.

Activity 11a

Lionel smiled. "It's hard to see how anything good could come from getting lost and needing a new home," he said. "Only a person with extra time on his hands. . ."

". . . who can't play baseball or swim or go to camp would have time to care for this dog!" finished Mario. "I could teach this dog lots of tricks, too. Mr. Nathan, this dog needs something good to happen for her, and I am hoping for something good to come from the change in my summer plans," cried Mario as he waved his cast for Mr. Nathan to see. "I'll take her!"

Mario knelt down to greet the dog. The eager puppy was happy to meet her knew friend. She licked his hands and his cheek. "Don't you think you should check with your mom and dad, first?" asked Mr. Nathan.

"Nah," said Mario. "I'll just remind them of the family motto: expect something good to happen! They're going to love our new friend."

Lionel rolled his eyes. He knew his parents weren't going to be happy with Mario's discovery, but how could Lionel argue with the family motto?

Activity 11a

Step 2 — Student Tips

- When you are asked to explain something, you are really being asked to answer WHY (the reason) and HOW (the process).

- Look for clues to tell you **why** the author is writing. For example, when nonfiction writing provides information, you may see facts, charts, graphs, and other data. Poetry or fiction is written for enjoyment; you may see descriptive words and entertaining sentences.

- You will be able to explain **how** the author tells the purpose for writing by writing down the sentences from the text.

Step 3 — Directions for using Reading Map 11a

First: Read the definition of the purpose for fiction, poetry, and nonfiction.

Second: Circle the type of writing in the box on the left (**fiction, poetry,** or **nonfiction**).

Third: Write the author's purpose in the box (why the story was written).

Fourth: Write a sentence or sentences from the story that show an example of the author's purpose (how the author tells the purpose for the writing).

©2002 Englefield & Associates, Inc.

Activity 11a

Map 11a

Explain How and Why an Author Uses Contents of a Text to Support His/Her Purpose for Writing

I tell the process (how) and the reason (why) the story was written.

Purpose of Fiction
- enjoyment and entertainment
- understand life, people, and experiences
- find out about the lives of the characters and how they are similar to you
- understand how characters solve problems that may be similar to yours

Circle the type of writing.

fiction
poetry
nonfiction

Tell why the story was written by writing the author's purpose for the story. (Pick an answer from the purpose boxes.)

_____

Purpose of Poetry
- enjoyment of the poet's feelings, expressive words and images
- understand the poet's thoughts about life
- find out about the subject
- solve problems in your life by comparing them to the poet's writing

Purpose of Nonfiction
- enjoyment
- understand something
- give information, facts, or data
- help you solve problems
- figure out how to do something
- persuade you to agree with the author

Write sentences from the text that show how the author tells the purpose for writing.

_____
_____
_____
_____
_____

©2002 Englefield & Associates, Inc.

Activity 11a

Step 4 Read the following questions and write your answers.

1. What is the type of writing in this story?

   _____
   _____
   _____

2. How did you figure out the purpose of the story?

   _____
   _____
   _____

3. Why was the story written? Explain how you figured out the answer.

   _____
   _____
   _____

4. Is the story successful in achieving its purpose? Give a reason for your answer.

   _____
   _____
   _____

©2002 Englefield & Associates, Inc.

Activity 11b

Explain How and Why an Author Uses Contents of a Text to Support His/Her Purpose for Writing

I tell the process (how) and the reason (why) the story was written.

Step 1 Read the announcement "Join the Bell Choir."

Join the Bell Choir

WHO IS INVITED?

You are invited to join the Cedartown Community Bell Choir. If you can count, you can play the bells. All ages are welcome.

WHAT WILL YOU DO?

After just a few practices, you will be ready to play with the bell choir. No experience necessary. We will teach you everything you need to know to be a bell ringer. And we supply the bells!

WHEN AND WHERE IS PRACTICE?

Our group practices every Tuesday afternoon from 3:00 p.m. to 4:00 p.m. at the community center located on Spruce Drive.

WHY SHOULD YOU JOIN?

Come and meet new friends and have fun. Free refreshments are served after practice. Please join us!

Activity 11b

Step 2: Student Tips

- When you are asked to explain something, you are really being asked to answer WHY (the reason) and HOW (the process).

- Look for clues to tell you **why** the author is writing. For example, when nonfiction writing provides information, you may see facts, charts, graphs, and other data. Poetry or fiction is written for enjoyment; you may see descriptive words and entertaining sentences.

- You will be able to explain **how** the author tells the purpose for writing by writing down the sentences from the text.

Step 3: Directions for using Reading Map 11b

First: Read the definition of the purpose for fiction, poetry, and nonfiction.

Second: Circle the type of writing in the box on the left (**fiction**, **poetry**, or **nonfiction**).

Third: Write the author's purpose in the box (why the story was written).

Fourth: Write a sentence or sentences from the story that show an example of the author's purpose (how the author tells the purpose for the writing).

©2002 Englefield & Associates, Inc.

Activity 11b

Map 11b

Explain How and Why an Author Uses Contents of a Text to Support His/Her Purpose for Writing

I tell the process (how) and the reason (why) the story was written.

Purpose of Fiction
- enjoyment and entertainment
- understand life, people, and experiences
- find out about the lives of the characters and how they are similar to you
- understand how characters solve problems that may be similar to yours

Purpose of Poetry
- enjoyment of the poet's feelings, expressive words and images
- understand the poet's thoughts about life
- find out about the subject
- solve problems in your life by comparing them to the poet's writing

Purpose of Nonfiction
- enjoyment
- understand something
- give information, facts, or data
- help you solve problems
- figure out how to do something
- persuade you to agree with the author

Circle the type of writing.

fiction
poetry
nonfiction

Tell why the announcement was written by writing the author's purpose for the announcement. (Pick an answer from the purpose boxes.)

_____

Write sentences from the text that show how the author tells the purpose for writing.

_____
_____
_____
_____
_____

80 ©2002 Englefield & Associates, Inc.

Activity 11b

Step 4 Read the following questions and write your answers.

1. What type of writing is the text?

   _____

   _____

   _____

2. What is the reason the text was written?

   _____

   _____

   _____

3. How did you figure out why the text was written?

   _____

   _____

   _____

4. Write a sentence from the text that showed you how the author told his or her purpose for writing.

   _____

   _____

   _____

©2002 Englefield & Associates, Inc.

Activity 12a

Identify Main Idea/Supporting Details
I figure out the overall idea and supporting details of the story.

Step 1 Read the poem "Snowflakes Fall."

Snowflakes Fall

Snowflakes falling on a winter day,
quiver, glimmer,
shimmer,
and float in a special way.

From the clouds, snowflakes fall,
slowly moving, swirling,
twirling, whirling
crystal balls.

Snowflakes sail around,
fluttering, puttering,
not even uttering
tiny bits of sound.

Lazily, round and round,
flakes skip, dip, flip,
drift, drift, drift
down to the ground.

©2002 Englefield & Associates, Inc.

Activity 12a

Step 2 — Student Tips

- First, ask yourself what each stanza is about. By answering this question, you will be able to figure out the topic of the whole stanza, and the main idea sentence should be easier to find.

- The **main idea** sentence tells the overall message about the topic of the stanza.

- **Detail sentences** will support the main idea and will explain or will give information about the main idea.

Step 3 — Directions for using Reading Map 12a

First: Tell what the whole poem is about.

Second: Write one sentence from the poem that tells the main idea of the poem.

Third: Write a sentence that supports the main idea in each of the three detail boxes.

©2002 Englefield & Associates, Inc.

Activity 12a

Map 12a
Identify Main Idea/Supporting Details
I figure out the overall idea and supporting details of the story.

What is the whole poem about?

What is the main idea of the poem? (Write the sentence that tells the overall message about the topic.)

_____
_____

Detail (Write one sentence that supports, explains, or gives information about the main idea.)	**Detail** (Write one sentence that supports, explains, or gives information about the main idea.)	**Detail** (Write one sentence that supports, explains, or gives information about the main idea.)
_____ _____ _____ _____ _____ _____ _____	_____ _____ _____ _____ _____ _____ _____	_____ _____ _____ _____ _____ _____ _____

©2002 Englefield & Associates, Inc.

Activity 12a

Step 4 Read the following questions and write your answers.

1. What is the poem about?

   _____

   _____

   _____

2. Write one sentence that tells you the main idea of the poem.

   _____

   _____

   _____

3. Write one sentence that gives information and supports the main idea of the poem.

   _____

   _____

   _____

4. Tell one way snowflakes fall on a winter day.

   _____

   _____

   _____

©2002 Englefield & Associates, Inc.

Activity 12b

Identify Main Idea/Supporting Details

I figure out the overall idea and supporting details of the story.

Step 1 Read the story "A Pioneer School."

A Pioneer School

A long time ago, pioneer children went to schools much different from schools today. Most pioneer schools had only one room for children of all ages from the farming community. The school had a fireplace or a stove that the teacher had to keep filled up with logs or coal in order to keep the building warm on cold winter days. The floors and benches in the schools were made from wood, which was probably chopped from trees nearby.

Children had different experiences in the pioneer school than we do in schools today. Young and old children studied next to each other or in small groups. Children used small chalkboards and chalk to write their answers while sitting at their desks. Lunch was never made at school, and the children would bring lunches from home. Although the children learned the same basics of reading, writing, and math that are learned by children today, they learned them in a very different environment.

©2002 Englefield & Associates, Inc.

Activity 12b

Step 2: Student Tips.

- First, ask yourself what each paragraph is about. By answering this question, you will be able to figure out the topic of the whole paragraph, and the main idea sentence should be easier to find.

- The **main idea** sentence tells the overall message about the topic of the paragraph.

- **Detail sentences** will support the main idea and will explain or will give information about the main idea.

Step 3: Directions for using Reading Maps 12b.1 and 12b.2

Read the first paragraph.

First: Tell what the whole paragraph is about. (Reading Map 12b.1)

Second: Write one sentence from the paragraph that tells the main idea of the story. (Reading Map 12b.1)

Third: Write a sentence that supports the main idea in each of the three detail boxes. (Reading Map 12b.1)

Read the second paragraph.

First: Tell what the whole paragraph is about. (Reading Map 12b.2)

Second: Write one sentence from the paragraph that tells the main idea of the story. (Reading Map 12b.2)

Third: Write a sentence that supports the main idea in each of the three detail boxes. (Reading Map 12b.2)

©2002 Englefield & Associates, Inc.

Activity 12b

Map 12b.1

Identify Main Idea/Supporting Details
I figure out the overall idea and supporting details of the story.

What is the first paragraph about?

What is the main idea of the paragraph? (Write the sentence that tells the overall message about the topic.)

_____
_____

Detail (Write one sentence that supports, explains, or gives information about the main idea.)	**Detail** (Write one sentence that supports, explains, or gives information about the main idea.)	**Detail** (Write one sentence that supports, explains, or gives information about the main idea.)
_____ _____ _____ _____ _____ _____ _____	_____ _____ _____ _____ _____ _____ _____	_____ _____ _____ _____ _____ _____ _____

©2002 Englefield & Associates, Inc.

Activity 12b

Map 12b.2 Identify Main Idea/Supporting Details
I figure out the overall idea and supporting details of the story.

What is the second paragraph about?

What is the main idea of the paragraph? (Write the sentence that tells the overall message about the topic.)
_____
_____

Detail (Write one sentence that supports, explains, or gives information about the main idea.)
_____
_____
_____
_____
_____
_____
_____
_____

Detail (Write one sentence that supports, explains, or gives information about the main idea.)
_____
_____
_____
_____
_____
_____
_____
_____

Detail (Write one sentence that supports, explains, or gives information about the main idea.)
_____
_____
_____
_____
_____
_____
_____
_____

©2002 Englefield & Associates, Inc.

Activity 12b

| Step 4 | Read the following questions and write your answers. |

1. What is the main idea of the first paragraph?

   _____

   _____

   _____

2. Write one sentence from the first paragraph that gives information about the main idea.

   _____

   _____

   _____

3. What is the main idea of the second paragraph?

   _____

   _____

   _____

4. Write one sentence that supports the main idea of the second paragraph.

   _____

   _____

   _____

©2002 Englefield & Associates, Inc.

Activity 13a

Respond to the Text

I tell my thoughts, feelings, experiences, or observations of something similar to what happens in the story.

Step 1 Read the story "The Birthday Surprise."

The Birthday Surprise

"Today is going to be a great day," thought Olivia. It was her birthday. Olivia quickly got out of bed and hurried downstairs for breakfast. She knew today was her special day, and someone would certainly say, "Happy Birthday." They always celebrated her birthday with hugs, presents, cake, and a birthday song. That did not happen on this day. No one in her family said anything about her birthday. Olivia thought they had forgotten. She felt disappointed. She finished her breakfast and walked to school.

On the way to school, Olivia saw her friends, Lu and Debbie. They talked about the skating show they saw at the park last night. They also talked about their homework. Lu and Debbie didn't say, "Happy Birthday," to Olivia either. This was the first time her friends had not remembered her birthday. "We always do things together on my birthday, so they must have forgotten," thought Olivia. Olivia was puzzled when her friends did not say anything about her birthday.

When Olivia got to school, she talked to lots of people in her class. She talked about a lot of things. Olivia was thinking everyone must have forgotten her birthday. There was even a birthday chart on the wall. For the rest of the day, Olivia was hoping someone would remember her birthday. She did not want to be rude by reminding her friends they had forgotten her special day.

Olivia walked home slowly by herself. She thought she might watch some TV or read a book to forget about how bad she felt. This was the first time no one even said, "Happy Birthday," to her on her birthday.

©2002 Englefield & Associates, Inc.

Activity 13a

When she got home, Olivia walked through the house. It was so quiet. She sadly went to the living room, then to the dining room looking for her mom. No one seemed to be home. As Olivia walked into the kitchen, she heard a loud, "Surprise!" The room was full of her friends and family. There were balloons, a cake, and presents. Best of all, everyone sang, "Happy Birthday." She was so happy to have this surprise party! Everyone was laughing about how they had pretended to forget her birthday. After the party was over, Olivia thought about how wonderful her friends and family were to plan such a special surprise party.

Activity 13a

Step 2 — **Student Tips**

- When responding to the text, you give your thoughts, feelings, personal experiences, or observations of things that are like things from the story.

- It is important to link your own feelings, thoughts, experiences, and observations to the text.

- Look to see if any of the characters' feelings, thoughts, actions, or ideas are similar to yours. The setting, events, or theme of the story may also relate to your feelings or experiences.

- Words that describe emotions are included in the Reading Map. Use these words to share how you feel about the story, the poem, the play, or the essay.

Step 3 — **Directions for using Reading Map 13a**

First: After reading the story, write **thoughts and feelings** you have had of a something similar to what happened in the story. (You may use your own "feeling words" or use the "feeling words" in the word box on the page below.)

Second: Write about your **experiences or observations** of a similar thing.

©2002 Englefield & Associates, Inc.

Activity 13a

Map 13a

Respond to the Text

I tell my thoughts, feelings, experiences, or observations of something similar to what happens in the story.

After reading the story, tell your thoughts and feelings of something similar that happened to you. Use your own feeling words or use the bank below to help you.

After reading the story, tell about experiences or observations you have had of a similar thing.

Bank of words to describe how you might feel

Happy
Glad
Pleased
Proud
Wonderful

Afraid
Frightened
Scared
Shaky
Worried

Angry
Enraged
Furious
Mad
Upset

Depressed
Down
Rotten
Sad
Tearful

94 ©2002 Englefield & Associates, Inc.

Activity 13a

Step 4 Read the following questions and write your answers.

1. What happened in the story that was different from what Olivia expected?

   _____
   _____
   _____

2. How would you feel if your friends surprised you with a birthday party? Why would you feel this way?

   _____
   _____
   _____

3. Why didn't Olivia remind anyone that it was her birthday? What would you have done?

   _____
   _____
   _____

4. Tell about a time you or someone you know was surprised by something that happened.

   _____
   _____
   _____

©2002 Englefield & Associates, Inc.

Activity 13b

Respond to the Text

I tell my thoughts, feelings, experiences, or observations of something similar to what happens in the story.

Step 1 Read the story "Shadow."

Shadow

Shadow is a two-year-old black Labrador retriever. She is a friendly dog who lives with a man named Jason. Shadow's best friends are Happy Cat and Herbie, a baby basset hound. Shadow enjoys running and playing with her friends. Most of all, she loves to travel with Jason.

Every morning, Shadow watches Jason get ready for his day. On the weekends, Jason takes Shadow and her friends, Herbie and Happy Cat, different places. They all hop into the truck, look out the window, and enjoy the ride.

One day, Shadow noticed that Jason had his camping gear packed. Jason looked worried and a little grumpy as he looked at the huge pile of camping gear in his truck. The truck was so full of camping gear, there was no room for Shadow and her friends. Shadow asked Happy Cat and Herbie to think of ways to solve the problem. Shadow knew she could not fit in the truck with all the camping gear. Happy Cat and Herbie were sad because they knew Shadow loved to go on trips. Shadow tried to stay calm and tried not to worry about missing the camping trip, but she was wondering who would take care of her while Jason was gone.

As the trip got closer, the pile of camping gear grew and grew. Jason seemed so excited. Shadow tried not to worry about missing the fun. Happy Cat and Herbie tried to comfort her. Shadow was wishing she could be included in the trip.

©2002 Englefield & Associates, Inc.

Activity 13b

The next day, Shadow noticed a large box on the top of the truck. Shadow's friends came over and watched Jason put all the gear inside of the box. He looked very happy now that he had solved the problem of where to put all the camping gear. Shadow also saw her favorite toys placed inside the truck. She knew there would now be room for her inside of the truck. Shadow felt so happy, she started to jump for joy.

Just then, Jason called Shadow to the truck. Happy Cat and Herbie were invited also. Everyone jumped in the truck. Away they went to the campsite. Shadow felt like the luckiest dog in the world. She knew Jason made an extra effort so she and her friends could take the trip together.

©2002 Englefield & Associates, Inc.

Activity 13b

Step 2 — Student Tips

- When responding to the text, you give your thoughts, feelings, personal experiences, or observations of things that are like things from the story.

- It is important to link your own thoughts, feelings, experiences, and observations to the text.

- Look to see if any of the characters' feelings, thoughts, actions, or ideas are similar to yours. The setting, events, or theme of the story may also relate to your feelings or experiences.

- Words that describe emotions are included in the Reading Map. Use these words to share how you feel about the story, the poem, the play, or the essay.

Step 3 — Directions for using Reading Map 13b

First: After reading the story, write **thoughts and feelings** you have had of a something similar to what happened in the story. (You may use your own "feeling words" or use the "feeling words" in the word box on the page below.)

Second: Write about your **experiences or observations** of a similar thing.

©2002 Englefield & Associates, Inc.

Activity 13b

Map 13b

Respond to the Text

I tell my thoughts, feelings, experiences, or observations of something similar to what happens in the story.

After reading the story, tell your thoughts and feelings of something similar that happened to you. Use your own feeling words or use the bank below to help you.

After reading the story, tell about experiences or observations you have had of a similar thing.

Bank of words to describe how you might feel

Happy
Glad
Pleased
Proud
Wonderful

Afraid
Frightened
Scared
Shaky
Worried

Angry
Enraged
Furious
Mad
Upset

Depressed
Down
Rotten
Sad
Tearful

©2002 Englefield & Associates, Inc.

99

Activity 13b

Step 4 — Read the following questions and write your answers.

1. As Jason packed for the trip, how did Shadow feel? Write how you would feel if you were not able to go on a trip.

   _____
   _____
   _____

2. Shadow enjoys running and playing with her friends. Write about two things you enjoy doing with your friends.

   _____
   _____
   _____

3. How did Shadow feel when she knew her friends would be able to go on the trip with her? How would you feel if you could take your friends on a trip?

   _____
   _____
   _____

4. Shadow knew Jason went to extra trouble to include her and her friends on the trip. Tell about your observation or experience of including someone.

   _____
   _____
   _____

Activity 14a

Evaluate and Critique the Text
I tell about the strengths and the weaknesses of what I read.

Step 1 Read the article "Electricity."

Electricity

Go turn on your radio, your TV, or your light. Guess what? You have started a parade. Yes, that's right, a parade of small electrons, pushing, bumping, and marching along. Did you know electricity is made of moving electrons? The energy of the moving electrons is called electricity. It is this energy that makes your radio, TV, or light turn on. You cannot feel the energy or see what it looks like. It makes no sound and has no color. However, you can see how electricity is used.

Here are several ways electricity is used.

In communication, electricity is used to power radios and televisions. Satellites circling the earth use electricity. Electricity powers our copy machines, fax machines, computers, and the equipment that prints our newspapers.

In our homes, we use electricity to wash our dishes and our clothes. We cook with ovens, microwaves, and toasters. Cooking is so much easier when we use electricity. Refrigerators and freezers cool our food and keep it from spoiling. Electric-powered heaters keep us warm in the winter, and air conditioners keep us cool in the summer, maintaining comfortable temperatures for us to live in.

In transportation, we use electricity to move people around all over the world. Elevators, subway cars, electric trains, and ships all use electricity to carry people to and from place to place. Traffic lights turn red, yellow, and green because of electricity.

©2002 Englefield & Associates, Inc.

Activity 14a

Most people think we are lucky to have electricity, but some people think we should not use so much of it. By using electricity, we change how we live our lives. We no longer have to walk as much as people once did. We no longer have to build a fire to keep us warm at night. If we didn't have electricity, people would not have radio and television, and they would read more and talk with each other more. What do you think about how we use electricity?

The next time you turn on a button or switch, remember that inside a single wire, electrons are marching along. Lots of electrons go through the wires marching, pushing, and moving to help you live the way you do today.

102 ©2002 Englefield & Associates, Inc.

Activity 14a

Step 2 — Student Tips

- You will use the Reading Map to determine whether you think the material supports questions asked by your teacher or parent.

- The Reading Map includes a chart for you to list the information that supports the question and the information that does not support the question.

- Then, you will critique the text and tell "why" by writing your opinion and answering the question.

Step 3 — Directions for using Reading Map 14a

First: Write the question your teacher provides in the middle box.

Second: List the strengths (information that supports the question).

Third: List the weaknesses (information that does not support the question).

Fourth: After reviewing the strengths and weaknesses, write the answer to the question.

©2002 Englefield & Associates, Inc.

Activity 14a

Map 14a

Evaluate and Critique the Text
I tell about the strengths and the weaknesses of what I read.

The strengths are...

The teacher-generated question is:

The weaknesses are...

After reading the strengths and weaknesses, the answer to the question is: _____

104

©2002 Englefield & Associates, Inc.

Activity 14a

Step 4 Read the following questions and write your answers.

1. Write one detail that supports using electricity for communication.

   _____
   _____
   _____

2. How would we benefit from not using electricity?

   _____
   _____
   _____

3. Do you think the author convinced you that the invention of electricity has helped people? Give a reason for your answer.

   _____
   _____
   _____

4. Write one detail that tells how electricity has helped people in their homes.

   _____
   _____
   _____

©2002 Englefield & Associates, Inc.

Activity 14b

Evaluate and Critique the Text

I tell about the strengths and the weaknesses of what I read.

Step 1 Read the story "Summer Job."

Summer Job

During the summer, Jose and Teresa earn money doing odd jobs and chores for people in their neighborhood. Jose likes to cut grass and to take care of pets while their owners are away. He cuts so much grass that his trimmers become dull. He buys animal treats for the pets, which he takes to them when they have been inside all day.

Teresa likes to help paint fences and to baby-sit. She only has a big paintbrush, so sometimes it is difficult for her to paint in small places. She painted her neighbor's decorative garden fence, and her parents asked her to paint the fence around the rose bushes. She baby-sits every afternoon for three hours. When she baby-sits, she takes small toys, books, and treats to entertain the children.

When the end of the summer draws near, Jose and Teresa notice the sun setting earlier each day and the nights feeling cooler. They are so glad they had their summer jobs because they were able to save money to buy the things they want. When Jose and Teresa decided to count their money, they had each earned more than two hundred dollars. Their parents said they each had to save half the money, but they could spend the other half on whatever they wanted.

The only thing Jose and Teresa do not like about working in the summer is they have less free time to do all the things they usually enjoy doing in the summer. They both wish they had more time to ride their bikes and play ball. However, after looking at all the money they earned, they both decided having summer jobs was a good way to spend their time.

©2002 Englefield & Associates, Inc.

Activity 14b

Step 2: Student Tips

- You will use the Reading Map to determine whether you think the material supports questions asked by your teacher or parent.

- The Reading Map includes a chart for you to list the information that supports the question and the information that does not support the question.

- Then, you will critique the text and tell "why" by writing your opinion and answering the question.

Step 3: Directions for using Reading Map 14b

First: Write the question your teacher provides in the middle box.

Second: List the strengths (information that supports the question).

Third: List the weaknesses (information that does not support the question).

Fourth: After reviewing the strengths and weaknesses, write the answer to the question.

Activity 14b

Map 14b

Evaluate and Critique the Text
I tell about the strengths and the weaknesses of what I read.

The strengths are...

The teacher-generated question is:

The weaknesses are...

After reading the strengths and weaknesses, the answer to the question is: _____

108 ©2002 Englefield & Associates, Inc.

Activity 14b

Step 4 — Read the following questions and write your answers.

1. Write one detail that **supports** children working in the summer.

   _____
   _____
   _____

2. Do you think you would want to work in the summer? Why?

   _____
   _____
   _____

3. Write one detail that **does not support** children working in the summer.

   _____
   _____
   _____

4. Did the author convince you that the children should have summer jobs? Explain your answer.

   _____
   _____
   _____

©2002 Englefield & Associates, Inc.

Activity 15a

Summarize

I tell the overall meaning of the text in my own words.

Step 1 Read the article "Levers: Simple Machines."

Levers: Simple Machines

Machines come in many shapes and sizes. When you think of a machine, you probably think of a large item, like a washing machine or a dishwasher. But machines can be small, too. Did you know that a pair of scissors is a machine? So are many other household items, such as can openers and screwdrivers. A machine is anything with fixed or moving parts that act together to do work. A machine is also something that changes the direction, the force, or the motion of something.

Levers are one type of machine. Levers are interesting machines because they make it possible to lift bigger things than you might normally be able to lift. If you go to the park, you might be able to find a lever machine to play on: a teeter-totter. How many times have you lifted your friends up high on a teeter-totter? You may have noticed you can even lift friends who are bigger than you. The reason you are able to lift them up so high is that you are using a machine called a lever.

Levers make pushing and pulling much easier, as well as making heavy things easier to lift. The part of the lever that decides how much you can lift is called the fulcrum. If you look closely at the teeter-totter, you will find a piece of wood or block under the middle of the board. That is the fulcrum, or the pivot point. Where you put the fulcrum will change the amount of weight you can lift with the lever. People have used lever machines, similar to teeter-totters, to move heavy things for centuries. Next time you are riding on a teeter-totter, remember that you really are using a machine!

©2002 Englefield & Associates, Inc.

Activity 15a

Step 2: Student Tips

You will use the Reading Maps to write the main idea of each paragraph, as well as the whole story, in your **own words**. Unimportant details are left out of a summary. A summary is not copying what is read word for word. A summary only includes the **main events**. Remember to stay on topic. You will write one sentence for every paragraph. For example, if the text has five paragraphs, you will write five summary sentences. To write a complete summary, remember the following sequence.

- Read the entire text.
- Read each paragraph, one at a time, and cross out the unimportant details. Highlight the important information within each paragraph, and write the important details. This will help you know what is important to include in your summary.
- Write one sentence from the paragraph that restates the main idea in your **own words**.
- Write the overall idea of the entire text in your **own words**.

Step 3: Directions for using Reading Maps 15a.1, 15a.2, and 15a.3

First: Write the important information from paragraph 1 onto Reading Map 15a.1.

Second: Rewrite the important information using your own words to tell the overall idea of paragraph 1. (Reading Map 15a.1)

Third: Repeat the first and second steps to include each additional paragraph. (Reading Maps 15a.1 and 15a.2)

Fourth: Use your **own words** to tell the overall idea of the **whole selection**. (Reading Map 15a.3)

©2002 Englefield & Associates, Inc.

Activity 15a

Map 15a.1

Summarize

I tell the overall meaning of what I read in my own words.

Detail phrases and/or sentences from the text

Write the most important information from paragraph 1. Leave out unimportant details.

Write the most important information from paragraph 2. Leave out unimportant details.

Summary sentences

Think about the most important information that you wrote. Now, use your own words to write one sentence that tells the overall idea of paragraph 1.

Think about the most important information that you wrote. Now, use your own words to write one sentence that tells the overall idea of paragraph 2.

112 ©2002 Englefield & Associates, Inc.

Activity 15a

Map 15a.2

Summarize

I tell the overall meaning of what I read in my own words.

Detail phrases and/or sentences from the text

Write the most important information from paragraph 3. Leave out unimportant details.

Summary sentences

Think about the most important information that you wrote. Now, use your own words to write one sentence that tells the overall idea of paragraph 3.

©2002 Englefield & Associates, Inc.

113

Activity 15a

Map 15a.3

Summarize

I tell the overall meaning of what I read in my own words.

Use your own words to write one sentence that tells the overall idea of the entire text.

114

©2002 Englefield & Associates, Inc.

Activity 15a

Step 4 Read the following questions and write your answers.

1. Write two details from paragraph one that describe a machine.

   _____
   _____
   _____

2. Write one sentence that summarizes the description of a lever.

   _____
   _____
   _____

3. Write the important details that tell you how levers are used.

   _____
   _____
   _____

4. Write a sentence that summarizes the text.

   _____
   _____
   _____

©2002 Englefield & Associates, Inc.

Activity 15b

Summarize

I tell the overall meaning of the text in my own words.

Step 1 Read the poem "Betty the Bird."

Betty the Bird

Betty the bird is the prettiest in town.
She likes to fly high and flutter around.
She flies up to the trees way up in the sky,
And sits in the trees with her head held up high.

Betty the bird has a soft, lilting voice;
Singing sweet songs is her favorite choice.
By day she sings out in a fun sing-along;
At night, she has dreams of singing her songs.

So don't be surprised if one day coming soon,
You hear Betty up in the trees, singing a tune.
And when you're outside, look for that pretty bird,
Singing the sweetest sounds you've ever heard.

116 ©2002 Englefield & Associates, Inc.

Activity 15b

Step 2 — Student Tips

You will use the Reading Maps to write the main idea of each stanza, as well as the whole poem, in your **own words**. Unimportant details are left out of a summary. A summary is not copying what is read word for word. A summary only includes the **main events**. Remember to stay on topic. You will write one sentence for every stanza. For example, if the text has five stanzas, you will write five summary sentences. To write a complete summary, remember the following sequence.

- Read the entire text.
- Read each stanza, one at a time, and cross out the unimportant details. Highlight the important information within each stanza, and write the important details. This will help you know what is important to include in your summary.
- Write one sentence from the stanza that restates the main idea in your **own words**.
- Write the overall idea of the entire text in your **own words**.

Step 3 — Directions for using Reading Maps 15b.1, 15b.2, and 15b.3

First: Write the important information from paragraph 1 (or stanza 1) onto Reading Map 15b.1.

Second: Rewrite the important information using your own words to tell the overall idea of paragraph 1 (or stanza 1). (Reading Map 15b.1)

Third: Repeat the first and second steps to include each additional paragraph (or stanza). (Reading Maps 15b.1 and 15b.2)

Fourth: Use your **own words** to tell the overall idea of the **whole selection**. (Reading Map 15b.3)

©2002 Englefield & Associates, Inc.

Activity 15b

Map 15b.1

Summarize
I tell the overall meaning of what I read in my own words.

Detail phrases and/or sentences from the text
Write the most important information from stanza
1. Leave out unimportant details.

Write the most important information from stanza
2. Leave out unimportant details.

Summary sentences
Think about the most important information that you wrote. Now, use your own words to write one sentence that tells the overall idea of stanza 1.

Think about the most important information that you wrote. Now, use your own words to write one sentence that tells the overall idea of stanza 2.

118 ©2002 Englefield & Associates, Inc.

Activity 15b

Map 15b.2

Summarize

I tell the overall meaning of what I read in my own words.

Detail phrases and/or sentences from the text

Write the most important information from stanza 3. Leave out unimportant details.

Summary sentences

Think about the most important information that you wrote. Now, use your own words to write one sentence that tells the overall idea of stanza 3.

©2002 Englefield & Associates, Inc.

119

Activity 15b

Map 15b.3

Summarize
I tell the overall meaning of what I read in my own words.

Use your own words to write one sentence that tells the overall idea of the entire text.

©2002 Englefield & Associates, Inc.

Activity 15b

Step 4 Read the following questions and write your answers.

1. What important detail from the first stanza in the poem tells you what Betty the Bird likes to do?

   _____
   _____
   _____

2. What important detail from the second stanza tells you what Betty the Bird enjoys doing?

   _____
   _____
   _____

3. Write a detail that tells how Betty sounds when she sings.

   _____
   _____
   _____

4. Write one sentence that summarizes what you may hear if you find Betty the Bird outside.

   _____
   _____
   _____

©2002 Englefield & Associates, Inc.

Activity 16a

Cause and Effect

I read to find out the reason why something happened and what happened.

Step 1 Read the article "Sailing with a Compass."

Sailing with a Compass

Can you imagine being out on a boat in the middle of the ocean? All you would see is endless water below you and endless sky above. How would you know what direction to sail? How would you find your way home? How would you know if you were continuing to sail in one direction and not just going around in circles? That's how it was for the world's first sea adventurers until they learned how to use the sky to help them find their way.

Early sailors knew certain things about the sky. They used the sun, the stars, and the moon to guide them where they wanted to go. By paying close attention and charting these things, they learned how to stay on course and not to get lost. As a result, sailors could tell what direction they were going. It took a lot of knowledge and practice to become good navigators, but over time, the sailors mastered this skill and could find their way almost anywhere.

Later, a tool called a compass was developed. Sailors put a magnet on a piece of cork to make a compass. The magnetized metal always pointed north. Knowing that the compass magnet always pointed toward the north, sailors learned to set courses by devising a system that divided the world up into parts called degrees. They could set a course based on how many degrees away from north they wanted to go. Compasses were more accurate in finding directions than the sky, so sailors got lost even less than before. Even today, with all kinds of high tech equipment, sailors continue to use compasses to find their way across the ocean.

Activity 16a

Step 2 — Student Tips

You will use the Reading Maps to understand the reason why something happens and what happens as a result.

- The **cause** is the action or the reason that makes something happen.

- The **effect** is the result.

- When you read to understand cause and effect, it can become tricky because there can be several causes or several effects. The most important thing for you to think about is there should be a clear connection between the cause and the effect.

- Look for **Key Words** to help you figure out if the statement is a cause or an effect. The key words are listed in Reading Map 16a.

Step 3 — Directions for using Reading Map 16a

First: Read the definition of cause and effect, as well as the **Key Words**.

Second: Read the example of a cause and effect statement.

Third: Write a sentence based on the story that tells the cause, then the effect.

Fourth: Write a sentence based on the story that tells the effect, then the cause.

©2002 Englefield & Associates, Inc.

Activity 16a

Map 16a

Cause and Effect

I read to find out the reason why something happened and what happened.

Look for key words that are clues to help you figure out if the statement is a cause or an effect.
Some of the key words that tell you why something happened (cause) are: **because, since.**
Some of the key words that tell you what happened (effect) are: **therefore, as a result.**

Example Sentences

Here is an example of a cause and effect sentence:
Because gold was discovered in the west (cause), many people moved to the west (effect).

Sometimes the order is reversed and the effect comes before the cause. Here is an example of an effect and cause sentence:
Many people moved to the west (effect) **because** gold was discovered (cause).

Fill in the blanks with the information from the text to figure out the cause and effect of what you read.

They used the sun, stars, and the moon to guide them.
CAUSE: why something happened (Reason/Action) _____

therefore

EFFECT: what happened (Result) _____

Sailors did not get lost.
EFFECT: what happened (Result) _____

because

CAUSE: why something happened (Reason/Action) _____

124

©2002 Englefield & Associates, Inc.

Activity 16a

Step 4   Read the following questions and write your answers.

1. What was the result of early sailors using the sun, the stars, and the moon to guide them?

   _____

   _____

   _____

2. Why are sailors today able to find the direction they want to go?

   _____

   _____

   _____

3. What were the results of sailors learning that magnetized metal always pointed north?

   _____

   _____

   _____

4. What is the reason sailors divided the earth into degrees?

   _____

   _____

   _____

©2002 Englefield & Associates, Inc.

Activity 16b

Cause and Effect

I read to find out the reason why something happened and what happened.

Step 1 Read the article "How Cars Changed Our World."

How Cars Changed Our World

Have you ever wondered how many things in our world have changed because of the invention of the car? Just take a ride down the street to see for yourself all the things that would be different if we did not have cars today. How many things can you think of that the invention of cars has changed in the world?

Although paved roads were developed well before cars were invented, they were not as common or as necessary as they are today. Early roads were sometimes paved with stones, logs, boards, or brick, but most roads remained dirt roads. The problem with dirt roads was they became very muddy when it rained. In earlier times, horses could easily travel on the muddy roadways, but the wheels of wagons and carriages often became stuck in the messy mud. As cars became more popular after World War I, people soon realized that the dirt roads that covered most of the country needed better surfaces. This was because the weight of the cars made it much more difficult for them to travel through muddy areas. Construction workers and engineers used asphalt, which created a hard, smooth surface, to pave many of the dirt roads. Soon, the number of paved roads began to grow, linking major cities together and making travel across the country easier. Today, there are many roads winding throughout the country, most of which are paved with asphalt. In fact, it is a rare sight to see a road that is not paved with anything.

Because roadways were becoming easier to travel on, people were able to get around more quickly than before. They were also able to travel more often. Before the invention of cars, it was not uncommon for people to stay very close to their homes for most of their lives. That changed when cars and improved roadways made travel simpler and quicker than before. It was common for people to go on Sunday drives where they would get to see places in the nearby countryside they had never seen before. The beautiful open spaces appealed to many people who lived in the city.

When cars became affordable for the average family, many people no longer had to live in the city to be close to where they worked. They realized they could move farther out of the crowded city and buy larger pieces of land at less expensive prices than in the city. Small towns near the bigger cities became residential communities, and the land in between was populated with people looking for their own pieces of land. Eventually, these communities came to be known as suburbs. People began to desert the cities, and shopping areas were built around the new areas where people lived. Even though the populations of cities were declining, the larger area of suburbs around the cities was growing, increasing the greater metropolitan areas.

The next time you are out riding in an automobile, look around you and imagine what the world would be like if there were no cars. You will be surprised at what you can come up with.

Activity 16b

Step 2: Student Tips

You will use the Reading Maps to understand the reason why something happens and what happens as a result.

- The **cause** is the action or the reason that makes something happen.

- The **effect** is the result.

- When you read to understand cause and effect, it can become tricky because there can be several causes or several effects. The most important thing for you to think about is there should be a clear connection between the cause and the effect.

- Look for **Key Words** to help you figure out if the statement is a cause or an effect. The key words are listed in Reading Map 16a.

Step 3: Directions for using Reading Map 16b

First: Read the general cause from the passage.

Second: List two effects of the cause.

©2002 Englefield & Associates, Inc.

Map 16b

Cause and Effect
I read to find out the reason why something happened and what happened.

Activity 16b

Cars were invented.

Cause: **why** something happened (Reason/Action)

As a result

Effect: **What** happened (result)

Effect: **What** happened (result)

©2002 Englefield & Associates, Inc.

129

Activity 16b

| Step 4 | Read the following questions and write your answers. |

1. What is one result that happened because cars were invented?

   _____
   _____
   _____

2. Write a second result that happened because cars were invented.

   _____
   _____
   _____

3. Why did cars need paved roads more than horses and buggies?

   _____
   _____
   _____

4. Why did the populations of cities begin to decline?

   _____
   _____
   _____

Activity 16c

Cause and Effect

I read to find out the reason why something happened and what happened.

Step 1 Read the article "The United States Becomes a Nation."

The United States Becomes a Nation

The United States has not always been the land of the free and the home of the brave. In fact, the United States has not always been the United States. Before the United States became a nation, it was a group of colonies ruled by the government and king in England. How did this country go from being a bunch of colonies to an independent nation?

At first, the colonists enjoyed a pleasant relationship with England. England allowed its people to travel to the colonies in order to promote the growth of the English empire. Colonists were expected to remain loyal to England, to pay taxes to the English government, and to supply England with resources found in the colonies. These resources included things such as lumber, tobacco, and other raw materials. The English would use these materials to make items to be sold at market in both Europe and the colonies.

At first, this relationship worked well for both the colonies and England. As the number of colonists grew, though, some colonists thought England was taking advantage of the colonies. In places like Virginia and Pennsylvania, people met to discuss the creation of an independent country. This new country would have its own laws and its own government and would be free from English rule.

A group of representatives from each of the 13 English colonies met to discuss the idea of independence. They decided to write down the reasons why they thought the colonies deserved to be free from England. This list of reasons was put into a document called the Declaration of Independence. Some of the reasons they listed talked about how they thought they were treated unfairly by the King of England and the English government. Other reasons talked about how they thought they deserved new freedoms. These freedoms are part of the American way today, but colonists did not have many rights or freedoms.

The colonists signed this declaration and sent it to the King of England himself. The English did not want to lose their colonies and did not think the colonists deserved the rights and the freedoms they wanted. The King of England sent soldiers to the colonies to prevent the colonists from gaining independence. A war began between the colonists and the English soldiers. This was the Revolutionary War. After a few years of fighting, the colonists won the war, and the English were forced to leave the colonies. The colonies soon united into a new nation which we know as The United States of America.

©2002 Englefield & Associates, Inc.

131

Activity 16c

| Step 2 | **Student Tips** |

You will use the Reading Maps to understand the reason why something happens and what happens as a result.

- The **cause** is the action or the reason that makes something happen.

- The **effect** is the result.

- When you read to understand cause and effect, it can become tricky because there can be several causes or several effects. The most important thing for you to think about is there should be a clear connection between the cause and the effect.

- Look for **Key Words** to help you figure out if the statement is a cause or an effect. The key words are listed in Reading Map 16a.

| Step 3 | **Directions for using Reading Map 16c** |

First: Read the general effect from the passage.

Second: List two causes of the effect.

132   ©2002 Englefield & Associates, Inc.

Activity 16c

Map 16c

Cause and Effect
I read to find out the reason why something happened and what happened.

[Cause: **Why** something happened (reason/action)]

The colonists formed a new nation.

Effect: **What** happened (result)

Because

[Cause: **Why** something happened (reason/action)]

©2002 Englefield & Associates, Inc.

Activity 16c

> **Step 4** Read the following questions and write your answers.

1. Write one reason from the text that tells you why a new nation was created.

   _____
   _____
   _____

2. Write another reason from the text that tells you why a new nation was created.

   _____
   _____
   _____

3. Why was it necessary for the colonists to fight the English?

   _____
   _____
   _____

4. Why did the colonists want a new government?

   _____
   _____
   _____

Student Notes

Student Notes

Student Notes

Thank YOU For Your Purchase!

For more information on our products, call 1-877-PASSING (727-7464), or visit our website:

www.showwhatyouknowpublishing.com